# MASTERING YOUR MOODS

# MASTERING YOUR MOODS

## UNDERSTANDING YOUR EMOTIONAL HIGHS AND LOWS

Paul Meier, M.D.,
Stephen Arterburn, M.Ed.,
Frank Minirth, M.D.

THOMAS NELSON PUBLISHERS
Nashville

Published in Nashville, Tennessee, by Thomas Nelson, Inc.

Unless otherwise noted, Scripture quotations are from THE NEW KING JAMES VERSION. Copyright © 1979, 1980, 1982, 1990, Thomas Nelson, Inc., Publishers.

Scripture quotations noted KJV are from the KING JAMES VERSION.

Scripture quotations noted NIV are from the HOLY BIBLE: NEW INTERNATIONAL VERSION®. Copyright © 1973, 1978, 1984 by International Bible Society. Used by permission of Zondervan Publishing House. All rights reserved.

Library of Congress Cataloging–in–Publication Data
Meier, Paul D.
    Mastering your moods : understanding your emotional highs and lows / Paul Meier, Stephen Arterburn, Frank Minirth.
      p. cm.
    Includes bibliographical references.
    ISBN 0-7852-7869-9 (hc)
    1. Affective disorders—Popular works. 2. Mood (Psychology)—Popular works. 3. Self-help techniques. I. Arterburn, Stephen, 1953– II. Minirth, Frank B. III. Title.
RC537.M44 1999
616.89'5—dc21

                  98–53506
                  CIP

*Printed in the United States of America*
1 2 3 4 5 6 BVG 03 02 01 00 99 98

To the billions who have suffered or died
as a result of needless, undiagnosed mood swings
over the course of human history.
—*Paul Meier, M.D.*

# CONTENTS

# PART 1

# IDENTIFYING
# YOUR
## MOODS

# 1 UNUSUAL HIGHS AND LOWS

Dr. Paul Meier led Peter and Wendy from the waiting area into his office. In their late twenties, both were dressed as if they had just come from office jobs, and by the personal data sheet the couple had filled out, Dr. Meier saw they had been married about four years.

Wendy caught Dr. Meier's eye first. Curiously, she looked both tired and elated—eyes wide but etched in red, skin ashen but very alive. She walked with a quick step, leading the way into the doctor's office.

Peter also looked tired, but his hands seemed very busy. They moved from his hair, to his chin, to his hair again, to brushing against his nose—giving the impression of weariness undergirded by a deeply rooted apprehension. "Thank you for seeing us on such short notice," he said apologetically. "This might be something of an emergency."

"Glad I was able to fit you in." They were now in Dr. Meier's office. Spacious and lined with books, it was both functional and comfortable. "You guys take the couch and I'll take the chair."

Instead of sinking into the couch, both perched on the edge. Peter sat nervously, as if there were questions he must ask and answers he was afraid to hear. Wendy seemed void of anxiety, but her muscles were tight, like a bird preparing to take flight.

Dr. Meier did not have to wait long for her to take off. As he was about to take the seat facing them, an emotional dam seemed to break somewhere inside her.

Wendy looked as if she had been holding her breath for several minutes and finally gulped for air. "I can't believe I did it," she gasped. "He told me that if I said another word before we got here, he'd divorce me. I did it." She grabbed his arm and gave it a squeeze. "I did it, didn't I do it, Peter. He likes me to call him Peter instead of Pete. Pete's too short. Pete. Pete." She said the name as if flicking it into the air. "He thinks there's something wrong with me, but I feel great. How can there be something wrong if I feel so great?"

Dr. Meier eased forward. "How long have you been like this—so happy?"

Peter answered, his tone measured, as if holding back a sea of emotions. "Three days now. She's up all night and generally driving me crazy. And the credit cards—I've had to hide them."

"But it's been wonderful. I've been so free, so creative. I'm a history teacher. Teaching is all I've ever wanted to do. And when I'm like this the ideas come so fast and so clearly, I could teach all day and all night. Do you like history, Dr. Meier?"

"Love it," Paul said. "Especially World War II. D-Day and all that."

"I like the Revolutionary War," Wendy said. "Seeing things that God did."

"Please do something," Peter pleaded.

"Tell me how you came to be a teacher," Paul said, giving Peter a look that asked him to have patience.

"I always wanted to teach. Even before I knew what I was going to teach, I knew I was going to teach something." She spoke quickly, her words springing up from an inexhaustible well.

"When I was a junior in high school, I finally decided on history. It was because of Mr. Stewart. I loved Mr. Stewart. He taught ancient history—the Greeks and Romans—and he gave me all the dos and don'ts about teaching history. Don't stress dates, do stress the flow of events. Don't change history to support a preconceived notion, do let history support what it supports. But if it doesn't support your preconceived notion, don't teach that part of it at all—just kidding."

She laughed at that, a solid, penetrating laugh. "In college I majored in U.S. history, and since I'm a Christian—another reason I know I'm in my right mind, God didn't make crazy people—I focused on God's work in the Revolution."

"When did you first have these elated feelings?" Paul asked.

Speaking even more rapidly than before, she began. "I guess the first time—yes, that was the first time. In the middle of teaching a class, I suddenly felt like I was injected with adrenaline. My energy level shot right up there. Gosh, it was fun. At first I didn't even know anything had changed. But then the kids started laughing and a couple of them asked questions, trying to mimic me. But I didn't care. Feeling this good, who would care."

"Then she got home," Peter went on. "And she couldn't sleep. I need my sleep. I'm an engineer—one mistake and a bridge falls."

Wendy threw a dismissing hand Peter's way. "But whether the bridge falls or not, the kids loved me and I loved it. I felt so free. Right in the middle of grading papers, I just picked them up and threw them across the room. Have you ever wanted to do that?"

"It might feel good," Dr. Meier said cautiously.

"It was great. The class and I laughed the whole time."

"Please, doctor," Peter said again. "The students call her Ms. Chimp."

"Oh, they do not," Wendy said, launching into a rapid list of reasons that could not be true—a list that went from "They love me" to "I'd kill them if I ever heard it."

"Some of the students told me," Peter said to Dr. Meier. "That's why we're here today. I heard you on the radio talking about things like this, and I decided it was time to come in."

"You just don't want me feeling happy," Wendy accused her husband. "You want me depressed all the time, don't you?"

"Are there depressions?" Dr. Meier asked.

"Sometimes," Wendy said, her eyes clouding. Then she seemed to reel a little, as if there had been an earthquake inside her. "Oh, I'm starting to feel tired."

"Tell me about the depression," Paul asked.

"It's horrible," Peter said. "Just horrible. I would keep asking God to bring her out of it, but He didn't seem to hear. I frankly don't know how she got out of the depression without killing herself—or me."

"I don't want to think about that right now," she said, her eyes growing weary again. She pinched the bridge of her nose. "I'm getting a headache, Peter. Lord, please don't let me have another one of those headaches. Oh, He never listens, anyway. I'm coming down, Peter. They don't call me Ms. Chimp, do they, Peter?"

"Dr. Meier." Peter's eyes became large with pleading. "I really can't take this anymore. And her principal is about to come unglued too. Isn't there anything you can do?"

Paul reached out with a comforting gesture. "I've only known you two for a few minutes, but I already see you are sensitive people who are dealing with something difficult, and dealing with it the best way you know how.

"Wendy, even though you feel very elated right now, you are talking very fast. Peter and I are both having a hard time breaking in, and your thoughts are racing. I think you probably have a mood disorder, a genetic one, that causes unusual highs and lows emotionally. If so, I'd like you to try taking some medication to bring you back to normal. You may also need to stay in our day program for a couple of weeks. But I need to ask some medical questions first, to be sure I'm correct. If everything points to that, are you willing to give treatment a try? I believe we can help level out your mood swings."

Both Wendy and Peter straightened perceptively, as if the hope in Paul's voice had given them a small, but welcome, boost. Wendy spoke first. "Okay, it's worth a try. If I keep doing this, one day soon I'll come home from school and find my bags packed on the front porch."

## EXPERIENCING UNUSUAL HIGHS AND LOWS

Have you ever experienced the kind of emotional highs Wendy was living through? Or the interminable lows, the depression she hates to even think about? Have you experienced moods that caused you to do things that hurt your reputation, or worse, that hurt those around you? Have you asked yourself what you could possibly do to work yourself out of your mood—your depression, your irritation—and found no answer?

Perhaps, like Wendy and Peter, you have wondered where God was. After all, He said He would never leave you nor forsake you. Yet that's what He seems to have done. God seems to be bouncing your emotions around like a Ping-Pong ball—perhaps even taking your very soul and wringing it dry of all feeling. And the question you keep asking remains conspicuously unanswered: If God loves me, if God is still here with me, where is the fulfillment and the real joy in life?

Doctors Paul Meier and Frank Minirth, nationally known psychiatrists, and Stephen Arterburn, founder and chairman of the New Life Clinics, have seen and studied hundreds of people just like Wendy. People trapped in the deserts of their emotions—incredible highs, deep depressions, and the roller coaster trip back and forth between them.

## MOODS AND MOOD SWINGS

Emotions are usually transient; they constantly respond to our thoughts, activities, and social situations throughout the day. Moods, in contrast, are consistent extensions of emotion over time, sometimes lasting for hours, days, or even months in the case of some forms of depression. Our moods color our experiences and powerfully influence the way we interact.

We all have moods. We wake up cranky or find ourselves depressed after something goes wrong at work or at home. Moods come and go, and when they do we are usually able to work our way out of them. We might pray, or count our blessings, or think about someone we love who returns that affection. And after a while we get back to normal.

But it is not always that easy. Sometimes we find ourselves at the mercy of our moods. A deep depression refuses to go away, and every time we try to evict it, it gets worse, becomes more entrenched. It starts affecting our lives and our relationships, our jobs, our church life. We find it hard to smile, hard to "look on the bright side," hard to even acknowledge there *is* a bright side.

Or we find ourselves on the opposite end of that spectrum, as Wendy did. Now, there are not many people who will complain about being too happy. In Wendy's case, it was her husband, Peter, who complained. But if you experience such elation, you know it. Maybe you're speaking too fast, or flitting about from place to place like a bird, or acting impulsively—doing things you would never think about doing normally. Maybe you're spending too much, running up big credit card bills for no other reason than you just want things. You may even impulsively seduce strangers. Maybe you're not sleeping for days at a time, and when you should be exhausted, you're wide awake and looking for new projects to tackle.

*And then you come down.* Either suddenly back to normal again, or you skip normal and plunge into depression.

Maybe you experience these highs and lows one right after another, in a cycle. Some people cycle like this every few years. Others are rapid cyclers, going through big mood swings every few months, or even every few weeks or days. A rapid cycler is someone who experiences four or more mood episodes—either lows or highs—per year.

## THE FALLOUT OF MOOD SWINGS

Not only do unusual highs and lows wreak havoc with the individual, as you can see from Wendy's experience, but they also place an unusual strain on those close to you, as with Peter. Normal conversation stops. Words and actions are studied but misunderstood. Anxiety and fear become predominant emotions. The focus of the relationship may shift to survival. And relationships cannot thrive very long in that mode.

Another relationship suffers amid these highs and lows— the relationship with God. To those reeling from a roller coaster ride of mood swings, God often becomes distant and disinterested, especially during depressive dips. They feel God has turned His back on them, no longer loves them, and has gone on to other things. Thinking that not even God loves them only deepens this sense of alienation.

You may be wondering just how many people suffer from moods and mood swings. More than you might imagine.

Those who, like Wendy, suffer from bipolar disorders (which we will discuss in detail later) number about eight million. When we add to that the number of Americans who suffer from a clinical depression—at any given moment approximately seventeen million people have depression that requires professional assistance to climb back to normal—we're now up to twenty-five million people who suffer from severe moods or mood swings. And that does not count those suffering from depressions that are not clinical—people who find themselves in prolonged emotional lows but who have found ways (such as following the methods described in this book) to get themselves back to normal. That number is impossible to know for sure, but current estimates place it at over fifty million people.

And, tragically, every year thirty thousand of the fifty million people who are depressed commit suicide.

But we do not want you to be dismayed by these statistics, for there *is* hope if you or someone you love is suffering from the emotional highs and lows of a bipolar or related disorder.

## HOPE FOR THE HURTING

As Dr. Meier told Wendy and Peter, professional counseling can take the sufferer to a place that is far more stable and satisfying. And because medical researchers have made grand strides in their understanding of the chemical makeup of the brain, medication—when coupled with an active counseling regimen—can bring the miracle of emotional stability and joy to those who have never known either.

So it was for Wendy. As you read this book you will see the work she did and the progress she made. For now, suffice it to say that she is currently leading a far more balanced, far more abundant life. Her husband is happier, and for the first time in her life, Wendy is experiencing real joy.

This book will map out the path that Wendy and others have taken, and if you find your own situation reflected in these pages, it will suggest a path you can take as well.

In Part 1 we will closely examine depression and identify other moods and mood swings. We will show that moods can be caused by external life issues—for instance, the loss of a job or a spouse. Or they can be caused by internal abnormalities—genetic factors or medical conditions. Part 1 will also take a look at what being on that mood swing roller coaster does to you and those around you. And we will explain what medications are available to treat depression, and how to know when you or someone you love needs medication.

Part 2 lays out a step-by-step process that, when followed, will take those suffering from externally caused moods and mood swings to a more balanced and fulfilled life. Genetic sufferers should take this journey too. As it turns out, those who suffer from genetic abnormalities experience at least as many mood-bouts as others, and often more, so following these steps can only help.

Part 3 will present the guidelines to happiness developed by Dr. Paul Meier and the seven keys to spiritual renewal taught by Stephen Arterburn. These spiritually grounded, commonsense principles have helped literally hundreds of thousands of people achieve wholeness and happiness. Implementing these principles in your life will act as an inoculation against future depressive episodes.

Part 4 presents the process to be followed by those afflicted with a bipolar spectrum disorder. We discuss managing this genetic condition with the proper medication and how family members can prepare to help the sufferer while protecting themselves from emotional damage.

Of course, completing any journey like this largely depends on you—your desire to extricate yourself from the emotional desert in which you find yourself, or to get off the emotional roller coaster taking you from high to low to high to low again. Even if you suffer from a bipolar or related disorder, you can make your life what God intends it to be. Our desire is always to be realistic and practical, and to make sure you have all the tools you need to set you on the road to wellness.

So let's begin. In the next chapter, we will take a closer look at various moods, starting with the most prevalent of all: depression.

# 2
# YOUR ENVIRONMENT AND YOUR MOODS:
## EXTERNAL FACTORS THAT CAUSE MOODS AND MOOD SWINGS

Although there seems to be an endless supply of moods and mood swings to choose from—depression, irritability, happiness, that sense of emotional soaring, grumpiness, etc.—moods and mood swings actually fall into only two major categories: those caused by external life issues, such as the death of a loved one or the loss of one's job; and those initiated by internal issues, such as medical conditions or genetic abnormalities. In this chapter we will take a closer look at moods caused by external life issues. In the following chapter we will tackle the internal issues.

In the first chapter we met Peter and his wife, Wendy, who was dealing with excessive emotional "highs." In this chapter we will start by examining the other end of the spectrum. Let's meet Melinda and Don, a couple dealing with depression.

## MELINDA AND DON

Dr. Paul Meier led Don and Melinda from the waiting room into his office and offered them the comfortable couch. They sat neither close to each other, nor at opposite ends. But when they were situated, their postures were very different. Melinda sank deeply into the cushions, appearing to let all her energy drain to some low, listless level. Don balanced on the edge, his energy encapsulated by the tight globe made by the fist of his right hand and his left hand closed over it.

Probably Melinda had once been a striking woman with penetrating cool blue eyes and soft auburn hair. Now her eyes seemed tired, and her hair was getting a little long and shaggy. Dr. Meier read the data sheet she had filled out and was surprised to see that she was in her late thirties. She looked older. She wore an expensive cream silk blouse and brown skirt, both a little small for her. Not overly so, but it appeared she was gaining weight and had not quite admitted it to herself. When she finally looked up, those eyes looked as if all the life had been beaten out of them; it was all they could do to stay open.

Don was a tall, lanky guy with a well-trimmed mustache. A little more alive, his life seemed concentrated in his impatient eyes. He wore a suit, probably having come straight from the office. If that were true, he made no attempt to hide the fact that he wanted to get back to work. But for all his restlessness there was a clear lack of spark in the man. Instead, he looked like someone who was being put through a wringer and who wanted desperately to be taken out of it.

After some brief amenities, Dr. Meier asked what brought them to his office.

Don achieved his goal. He spoke first. "She's depressed. I mean really depressed, and I'm getting to the point where I can't take it anymore."

Melinda had remained expressionless through Don's opening. "Is that true? Are you depressed, Melinda?" Paul asked.

"I guess," she said, offering far more information with her lifelessness.

"So you're here because your husband wants you here?"

"No," Don injected. "I'm only here because I thought I should be."

"My sister suggested it," Melinda offered. "She listens to you on the radio."

"What prompted her to suggest coming to see me?" Dr. Meier asked.

Melinda sighed, as if exhaling air would somehow pave the way for the words that had no intention of coming out on their own. "Jealousy," she quipped with heavy sarcasm. "She wants to be a stick-in-the-mud too."

"Jokes," Don groaned. "She comes here and makes jokes."

Dr. Meier kept his attention on Melinda. "Is that what you think you are? A stick-in-the-mud?"

"I'm the stick, the mud, everything."

"Have you always been?"

"No, she hasn't," Don said, bringing his perch even farther forward.

Dr. Meier raised a gently restraining hand. "I think it best if I hear it from her right now."

"No," Melinda said, still working from dying embers of strength. "Not always."

Dr. Meier put his hand on a pen and prepared to start taking notes. "When did you become a stick-in-the-mud?"

"A couple of months ago," Don said. Quickly realizing that he had interrupted by answering, he finally abandoned his perch and slipped back into the couch, crossing his arms.

"What were you like before that?"

"Active," Melinda said. "Really active. Get-up-and-go, that was me."

"In what setting were you so active—home, work, school?"

"I'm a domestic goddess—"

Dr. Meier smiled.

"A homemaker and mother. I've always volunteered to help the kids at school. I've always kept an immaculate house, and I did crafts—porcelain dolls, those puffy photo albums. I read a lot."

"But . . ."

"But," she sighed, "that's all changed. Now I don't feel like doing anything."

"Anything?" Dr. Meier asked.

"I don't want to clean the house anymore. I haven't vacuumed in two weeks. Clothes get washed and folded but not put away. Who wants to put clothes away, anyway. You just take them out again. And I haven't made the bed in over a month. I just don't want to do it. Like I don't want to do the bills anymore. I've done them for fifteen years and I don't want to anymore. At the end of every month I would gather them all together, write all the checks, balance the books—everything. No more." She took a labored breath. "I don't want to do anything. I don't even want to take the kids to school in the morning, or make their lunches, or go to those stupid school meetings . . ." She hesitated, then continued. "Or make love to Don anymore."

"She's really following through on that one," Don complained.

"Right now the only thing I feel right about is killing myself."

Dr. Meier became very serious. "It's common to feel that way when you're depressed. But God put you here for a reason—a divine purpose. When your job is done He'll take you home, as He does with all of us sooner or later. As you recover from your depression these suicidal feelings will fade away. So I want you to promise me that if you feel the urge to commit suicide, you'll call me or your counselor first to discuss it."

"Okay, you win. I'll live through this session at least." She managed a shallow smile.

"So what happened a couple of months ago that might have started your tailspin?" Dr. Meier asked.

"She blames me for it," Don piped up again.

Dr. Meier nodded toward him. "How?"

"I got a little down. Things were going badly at work. There was a lot of stress."

"And that spilled over to your home life?" Dr. Meier asked.

"Yes," Don answered simply. "It spilled over. I got a little irritable at home. Said some things that I shouldn't have said."

"And you're still saying them," Melinda fired at him, her energy suddenly spiking.

"But I'm coming to the end of my rope here."

Dr. Meier intervened. "Would you say your feeling of being down has passed?"

"Pretty much. There's still a lot of stress, and Melinda doesn't make it any easier. But I'm not as down as I used to be."

Dr. Meier wrote a note to himself then turned his attention to Melinda. "Melinda, do you talk to God? Do you maintain a relationship with Him?"

"Since I was a teen. But God seems so far away. So very far away. I'm wondering if He even exists anymore. Maybe God did die."

Dr. Meier's heart tightened. But then he smiled warmly at Melinda. "First, let me reassure you. God is alive and well, and He loves you deeply. Let me also assure you that depression like yours, what we call major depression or clinical depression, is nearly always curable with the right kind of help and direction, if you will also do your part in the process. From the sounds of things, your depression is probably environmental, but we'll confirm that soon. But in any case, you'll feel a lot better in a few weeks."

Dr. Meier glanced down at the note he had made: Don's minor depression probably caused Melinda's major depression.

Let's take a look at these moods.

## MINOR DEPRESSION

Minor depression is a feeling of melancholy that lasts for a little while and is caused by a tragic or potentially threatening event, or an important loss in the sufferer's life.

We all have moods and mood swings. There are times when everything is going great—our relationship with God is good, our relationship with our spouse is humming along, our kids are all behaving reasonably, everything happening at work is positive and, because of all that, we're happy—maybe even walking on air. Then something happens. Maybe a son or daughter gets in serious trouble, or we find out we're in line for a layoff at work—and suddenly we're plunged into worry, self-doubt, and depression.

Not one of us wants to cure that feeling of happiness, that all's-right-with-the-world glow that comes along. We would all prefer that particular feeling never end. But depression, even minor depression, is another thing altogether.

How can you tell if you are suffering from minor depression? Take this short test for guidance. (Circle T for true or F for false.)

    T  F    I feel sad most of the time lately.

    T  F    I'm usually a happy, energetic person, but I've felt more tired and irritable lately.

    T  F    There seems to be a single, identifiable event that caused my sadness.

    T  F    I seem to feel angry or guilty much of the time lately.

    T  F    I'm not suicidal, but I wouldn't mind that much if God told me to come home to heaven right now.

T  F    I've had this level of sadness before and have worked my way out of it without the help of medication or alcohol.

If you circled five or more Ts, you are probably suffering from a minor depression.

Minor depression is just the first example of moods and mood swings we will cover in this book. The next one is a feeling that always seems to stop just short of happiness.

## Environmental Dysthymia

Dysthymia is a low-grade chronic depression and it describes a life like Warren's.

Warren is twenty-eight and it seems he never feels really happy. It's not that he's always depressed; depressions only come now and then. But he seems to feel a couple of notches below a normal sense of contentment. Even at parties, or right after getting a raise a work, he seldom feels happy. In fact, he senses something inside keeping the cork tightly in his "happiness" bottle.

### Dysthymic Disorder

A mild to moderate, chronic, persistent depression lasting two or more years (one year in adolescents).

Dysthymia occurs in 6 percent of people, can be genetic and/or environmental, and often begins in the twenties and thirties but may be lifelong.

A. While depressed, two (or more) of the following are present:

- poor appetite or overeating
- insomnia or hypersomnia (can't stay awake)
- low energy or fatigue
- low self-esteem
- poor concentration or difficulty making decisions
- feelings of hopelessness

B. During the two-year period (one year for children and adolescents) of the disturbance, the person has never been without the above symptoms for more than two months at a time.

C. No major depression has been present during the past two years of the disturbance, although it may or may not have started with a major depression.

D. There has never been a manic episode.

E. The disturbance is not caused by the taking of a chemical substance.

F. The symptoms cause clinically significant distress or impairment in social, occupational, or other important areas of functioning.

Of course, his job doesn't help much. Warren works at the headquarters of a car company on a customer service desk—their complaint department. People say it fits his personality. He comes to work in the morning, listens to people complain about their cars all day long, then goes home at night. Happiness is never demanded of him and when depression comes, he places the blame on work. Over time he comes back to what is normal for him—that gnawing sense of incompleteness, of disconnectedness.

There was a time when he responded to a Baptist altar call. And if you were to ask him, he would call himself a Christian. But when the pastors and other Christians talk about "the joy of the Lord," it's as if they are talking about things that happen on other planets and definitely to other people—not him.

Warren suffers from dysthymia. Although he has been this way as long as he can remember, the dysthymia sufferer need only have the symptoms for two years to be considered dysthymic. And what are those symptoms? They are Warren's.

Those suffering from dysthymia seldom if ever experience happiness, and there's a sense that something is keeping it from them. Like everyone, they also suffer from occasional bouts of worsening depression, but because their depressions start from a depressed normalcy, their depressions seem to go a little deeper than others suffering from the same malady.

They do suffer from what seems like an emotional paradox: although they sense that something inside them is keeping them from experiencing happiness, the cause of their dysthymia is either genetic or else it centers on their external relationships and how they have come to handle them. When we discuss the process which leads to wellness, we will take a closer look at the reasons for Warren's emotional situation.

What about you? Do you think you might be suffering from dysthymia? Take the following test for guidance. (Circle T for true or F for false.)

T  F  I have been feeling somewhat sad and discouraged for so long now that it seems like "normal" to me, until I see how happy some of my peers seem to be.

T  F  I have been more unhappy than most of my peers for two or more years now.

T  F  I have had trouble falling asleep or else falling back to sleep if I wake up during the night for most of the nights for two years or longer (without sleeping medications).

T  F  I often feel discouraged or even despondent, especially as each day wears on.

T  F  I have other emotional problems besides my chronic mild to moderate depression, such as perfectionism, relationship problems, oversensitivity, etc.

T  F  I can function adequately at home or at work, but I have some degree of chronic fatigue and have had to push myself for two or more years.

T  F  I have had frequent headaches or other physical symptoms that keep coming back periodically for two or more years now.

T  F  *I have one or more genetic relatives who have experienced a mood disorder.

T  F  *I have one or more genetic relatives who have been prone to major depressions during crises in their lives.

T  F  *I have one or more genetic relatives who have been chronically unhappy or fatigued for two or more years.

If you circled five or more Ts, then you may very well have dysthymia. If among those answered T are some marked with an asterisk (*), then your dysthymia may be primarily a genetic dysthymia, which will be covered in the next chapter.

## MAJOR DEPRESSION

Major depression is a deep, pervasive melancholia that saps both spirit and energy and seems to cover the sufferer's life in a thick, oppressive pall.

We met Melinda at the beginning of this chapter and she is suffering from major depression. Although her life was moving along smoothly, something happened, something outside of herself, something that caused her to take an emotional nosedive. And we've learned that the something concerned her husband and his minor depression. Where she had been a happy, active woman, committed to the well-being of her family, now she is a woman without direction, listless, struggling to get through each day as if swimming through thick molasses, often wishing the molasses would just swallow her up, delivering her from her misery.

### Major Depressive Episode

Depression lasting from fourteen days to several years and severe enough to cause great difficulty functioning at home, at work, or at school.

A major depressive episode may be accompanied by wishes of death or even suicidal thoughts. Some people are so depressed they become psychotic, with paranoid or grandiose delusions and/or auditory hallucinations (hearing negative voices that seem audible and real).

A. Five (or more) of the following symptoms have been present during the same two-week period (or longer) and represent a change from previous functioning; at least one of the symptoms is either (1) depressed mood or (2) loss of interest or pleasure. None of the symptoms are the result of medication or a medical condition.

  • Depressed mood most of the day, nearly every day.

- Marked diminished interest or pleasure in all, or almost all, activities most of the day, nearly every day.

- Significant weight loss when not dieting or weight gain (more than 5 percent of body weight in a month) or increase or decrease in appetite nearly every day. In children, it may show up as a failure to make expected weight gains.

- Insomnia or hypersomnia nearly every day.

- Psychomotor agitation (restlessness) or retardation (listlessness) nearly every day (this is observable and not just a subjective feeling).

- Fatigue or loss of energy nearly every day.

- Feeling of worthlessness or excessive or inappropriate guilt nearly every day.

- Diminished ability to think or concentrate, or indecisiveness, nearly every day.

- Recurrent thoughts of death (not just fear of dying), recurrent suicidal ideation without a specific plan, or a suicide attempt, or a specific plan for committing suicide.

B. The symptoms cause clinically significant distress or impairment in social, occupational, or other important areas of functioning.

C. The symptoms are not due to taking a chemical substance.

When major depression comes there is no mistaking it. It feels like the greatest of funks, but there is so much more than just feeling deeply blue; there is actual despair and hopelessness. Suicidal thoughts mingle with excessive feelings of guilt and shame, yet there is also an extreme lack of energy, which makes doing anything to rectify those feelings nearly impossible. As you can imagine, there is a decrease in the sex drive and with it a loss of self-worth, which is aggravated by the never ending stream of self-critical thoughts. You get the idea. And as you can imagine, dealing with major depression takes effort, and it may take medication.

What about you? Do you think you may be suffering from a major depression? Take the following test for guidance. (Circle T for true or F for false.)

T  F    I have felt very sad nearly every day for two weeks or longer.

T  F    I have lost interest in my usual activities.

T  F    I have had a significant change in my appetite (increase or decrease).

T  F    *I feel tired most of the time now and it has become very difficult for me to keep up with my usual daily activities.

T  F    I wake up halfway through the night and have trouble getting back to sleep.

T  F    *I sleep too much.

T  F    *I have been more irritable, agitated, and/or restless for awhile.

T  F    I have trouble concentrating and remembering things.

T   F    *I feel like I wish I could die at times.

T   F    I obsess about mistakes I have made.

If you circled five or more Ts, particularly those marked with an asterisk (*), you may be suffering from a major depression. And if you have thought seriously about suicide, turn to Chapter 5 right now and please reconsider those feelings.

We will follow Melinda and Warren through the process that leads them back to a fulfilling life. But for now, let's go on to the next stop on our journey. In the following chapter we will cover information about moods and mood swings caused by medical issues and genetic, or inherited, factors.

# 3 YOUR HEREDITY AND YOUR MOODS:

## MEDICAL CONDITIONS AND GENETIC FACTORS THAT CAUSE MOODS AND MOOD SWINGS

In the previous chapter, we looked at the moods and mood swings caused by a person's reaction to external, or environmental, situations. In this chapter, we are going to look at those caused by medical conditions and genetics. All but one of the genetically caused disorders we will examine belong to the bipolar spectrum disorders. This family includes any genetic (inherited) factors that cause lifelong mood swings too high or too low. They may start in childhood or not until the individual is well into his or her thirties, but seldom start after age forty. The ones we will cover in this chapter are ADHD (and ADD), genetic dysthymia, cyclothymia, and bipolar I and II.

Let's start, though, with a medically caused disorder that probably afflicts more than half of the women in America.

## PREMENSTRUAL SYNDROME (PMS) AND PREMENSTRUAL DYSPHORIC DISORDER (PMDD)

From 40 to 70 percent of menstruating women experience mood swings. If you are one of these, every month you sense yourself entering a tunnel of depression, anxiety, and irritability—and you enter it with bloating, tender breasts, and a craving for carbohydrates. By any measure, this time is uncomfortable and causes both you and those close to you some anxious times.

However, 3 to 8 percent of women develop an even more disabling variation of PMS known as premenstrual dysphoric disorder (PMDD). PMDD is typified by at least one of the following:

- sudden tearfulness or sadness

- marked irritability or anger that seems to persist

- marked feelings of edginess, tension, or anxiety

- marked self-critical thoughts, feelings of hopelessness, and depressed mood

Added to one of the above, the PMDD sufferer usually will have several of the following symptoms: feeling overwhelmed, trouble concentrating, breast tenderness, headaches, bloating, joint pain, muscle pain, weight gain, insomnia or hypersomnia, binge eating, craving specific foods, lethargy, lack of energy, easy fatigability, and/or decreased interest in usual activities.

But that's not the worst of it. After treating PMS and PMDD patients for many years, we have found that these disorders seem to be more common and much more severe among women who have been victims of childhood sexual abuse, rape, or even chronic emotional or physical childhood abuse. In other words, it appears that environmental factors can worsen an otherwise genetic/medical condition such as PMS or PMDD.

The good news in all of this is that there are treatments. In fact, new and more effective medications are being formulated all the time, and if you do suffer from PMS or PMDD, you should consult a physician to get the latest information.

## CURRENT TREATMENTS

Some women can be treated with progesterone or other hormone therapy, but many require antidepressant medication. The new SSRI (Selective Serotonin Reuptake Inhibitor) antidepressants result in normal happiness ratings in 64 to 88 percent of PMS and PMDD patients, as well as a 50 percent or greater reduction in the other symptoms in 60 to 65 percent of patients. Women who need SSRIs should take them every day throughout the cycle but should consult with their physician about possibly stopping prior to getting pregnant, just to be safe. Some OB-GYNs will carefully continue some of the SSRI antidepressants even during pregnancy, if needed, but we do not usually give meds to any pregnant woman.

## OTHER CONDITIONS THAT RESULT IN MOODS AND MOOD SWINGS

Since we are largely chemical creatures, chemical imbalance can have a lot to do with how we feel and the moods we experience. A number of different medical conditions can cause moods and mood swings, so one of the first things you might want to do is to have your physician perform a blood evaluation to see if you have one of the following conditions:

- anemia

- hypo- or hyperthyroidism

- electrolyte imbalances

- folate (folic acid) deficiency

- vitamin B-12 deficiencies

Even the flu, infectious mononucleosis, and many other physical illnesses can cause moderate to severe mood swings.

## BIPOLAR SPECTRUM DISORDERS

The next series of mood swing disorders are called the bipolar spectrum disorders. *Bipolar* describes the way the sufferer's emotions seem to gather around two opposing poles—depression and elation (or mania). The spectrum of these disorders begins with minor emotional swings and spans the gamut to the very severe.

Interestingly enough, the first disorder we will look at does not actually fall into the category of a mood or mood swing, but if you or someone dear to you has it, there is a heightened possibility of developing a bipolar spectrum disorder later in life.

## ADHD

Attention deficit hyperactive disorder is more like a kissing cousin of the bipolar disorders.

Those suffering from ADHD have trouble concentrating; ideas come and go, quickly replaced by new ones. They find it very difficult to sit and listen to a lecture of any length. They have difficulty sitting still. The person feels the need to be active. Often there is difficulty sleeping. The sufferer might have trouble falling asleep and certainly staying asleep. That's why it is so difficult on school-age children. The disorder flies in the face of an orderly education process.

---

### Attention Deficit Hyperactive Disorder

A genetic, lifelong disorder that begins in early childhood and is marked by impulsive behavior, distractibility and/or hyperactivity.

Males with ADHD are more likely to be hyperactive, while females are more likely to be easily distracted.

---

With ADHD there may or may not be mood swings. The *H* in ADHD refers to hyperactivity, so it can appear that the ADHD sufferer is having a mood—one of elation and high activity—but in fact, the sufferer may not be. It differs from a mood-high in several ways: early onset (i.e., before seven years of age); its chronic nature rather than episodic; its lack of clear onsets and offsets; and absence of expansive or elevated mood. In any case, ADHDs seem to be genetically connected to those who suffer from bipolar disorders. Those with ADHD have a higher than normal probability of experiencing one of the bipolar spectrum disorders later in life, resulting in pronounced and identifiable mood swings.

But ADHD sufferers can also be high achievers when properly treated. They have a lot of energy and are often quite creative, which is true of nearly all bipolar people.

What about you? Do you think you suffer from ADHD? Let's see what the following test says. (Circle T for true or F for false.)

T F  When I was in elementary school, I was often looking out the window or was otherwise distracted when the teacher called on me.

T F  I tend to be more impulsive than most people.

T F  I have trouble remembering more than one task at a time.

T F  I tend to be more restless and hyperactive than most people and have been so all my life.

T F  I have trouble concentrating on my task at hand unless it's a video game or something similar.

T F  I have trouble paying attention to teachers or preachers.

T   F   I tend to lose my temper more quickly than most of my friends and relatives.

T   F   I don't seem to handle stress as well as most people do.

T   F   I have one or more learning disabilities.

T   F   I tend to use prescription or illegal drugs and/or alcohol to slow myself down when I feel hyper.

If you answered true on five or more questions, then you may have one of the types of ADHD. If you now have children or sometime will, keep an eye out for possible bipolar spectrum behavior in them. They have a somewhat greater chance of experiencing it than the general population.

## GENETIC DYSTHYMIA

Genetic dysthymia is a chronic depression that looks just like the environmental dysthymia described in the last chapter, except that it lacks a specific external cause. The worst manifestation of this disorder is a life of feeling disconnected. We all need to love and be loved in honest relationships with God and people. Dysthymia, whether genetic or not, largely prevents that from happening.

Because the cause is genetic, a condition of all the bipolar spectrum disorders, someone suffering from genetic dysthymia may very well come from a good Christian family, has been loved, has never been abused or experienced any other life-changing traumatic event, or if the sufferer has, he or she has dealt with it successfully. By all rights, the genetic dysthymia sufferer should be living a life filled with normal ups and downs, with normal spikes of elation and normal blips of depression.

Instead, he or she travels life several notches below happiness; his joy would be described as an absence of depression, her laughter might sound like someone else's sigh.

That does not mean that genetic dysthymia may not be aggravated by external stressors; a genetically caused depression can always be made worse by something that depresses from the outside. But generally these people live depressed lives for no discernible reason at all.

What about you? Do you think you might be suffering from genetic dysthymia? Take the following test for guidance. Although this is the same test given earlier for what might be called environmental dysthymia, these disorders must be diagnosed by a physician and cannot be determined for sure from this test. (Circle T for true or F for false.)

T  F  I have been feeling somewhat sad and discouraged for so long now that it seems like "normal" to me, until I see how happy some of my peers seem to be.

T  F  I have been more unhappy than most of my peers for two or more years now.

T  F  I have had trouble falling asleep or else falling back to sleep if I wake up during the night for most of the nights for two years or longer (without sleeping medications).

T  F  I often feel discouraged or even despondent, especially as each day wears on.

T  F  I have other emotional problems besides my chronic mild to moderate depression, such as perfectionism, relationship problems, oversensitivity, etc.

T    F    I can function adequately at home or at work, but I have some degree of chronic fatigue and have had to push myself for two or more years.

T    F    I have had frequent headaches or other physical symptoms that keep coming back periodically for two or more years now.

T    F    *I have one or more genetic relatives who have experienced a mood disorder.

T    F    *I have one or more genetic relatives who have been prone to major depressions during crises in their lives.

T    F    *I have one or more genetic relatives who have been chronically unhappy or fatigued for two or more years.

If you circled five or more Ts, you may have dysthymia. If among those answered T are those marked with an asterisk (*), then your dysthymia may be genetically caused and be a member of the bipolar spectrum disorders.

Before we go on we need to define a couple terms, both having roots in the word *mania*.

## HYPOMANIA (OR HYPOMANIC EPISODE)

Hypomania is a mild feeling of euphoria that falls short of a full-blown manic episode. A person who is hypomanic has more to say than time and words to say it, so he talks fast, interrupts, and dominates the conversation. Ideas fly at him like hail and the only limit to his creativity seems to be the speed at which he thinks. And because time becomes an enemy, there is no time to sleep or even rest. There is also a loss of inhibition which causes the sufferer to succumb to impulses, even those of a sexual nature.

### Hypomanic Episode

A feeling of euphoria that can be anywhere from mild to extreme.

A.  A distinct period of persistently elevated, expansive, or irritable mood, lasting throughout at least four days, that is clearly different from the usual nondepressed mood.

B.  During the period of mood disturbance, three (or more) of the following symptoms have persisted (four if the mood is only irritable) and have been present to a significant degree:

- inflated self-esteem or grandiosity

- decreased need for sleep—rested after three hours of sleep

- more talkative than usual or pressure to keep talking

- flight of ideas or feeling that thoughts are racing

- easily distracted to irrelevant, unimportant things

- increase in goal-directed activities (either social, work, school, or sexual) or psychomotor agitation

- excessive involvement in pleasurable activities that have a high risk of painful consequences (e.g., buying sprees, sexual indiscretions, or foolish business investments)

C. The behavior is clearly uncharacteristic of the individual.

D. The behavior is observable by others.

E. The episode is not severe enough to include psychotic features (loss of reality base) and the hypomanic will maintain some limited ability to function socially and occupationally.

F. The symptoms are not due to the taking of a chemical substance.

Hypomania may include patches of irritability and extreme impatience—a feeling of moving faster and thinking more clearly than anyone else, and he wishes they would either catch up or get out of the way. But for all this activity and rapid thought, he never loses track of reality—who he is, what he is doing, and why he is doing it. And this pattern of behavior lasts at least four days.

## MANIA (OR MANIC EPISODE)
Mania includes all of the above, but the manic episode is severe enough to cause significant occupational or sociological impairment. It also is severe enough to cause problems with relationships. Worse yet, for a period of time, the sufferer might lose contact with reality. She might think she is God or that she has a special message to save the world. She might think she's an angel on an important mission. When the person comes back to reality, she remembers what she has done and is embarrassed.

With those two definitions in our tool kit, let's take a look at the moods and mood swings that include them. The first is cyclothymia.

## Cyclothymia

Cyclothymia is the mildest of the bipolar spectrum disorders—minor depression at one pole, and hypomania, or mild elation, at the other, neither with an external cause.

Let's meet Brenda, who suffers from cyclothymia. She and her husband, Jake, are both tall, willowy people. They met at a freshman retreat sponsored by Campus Crusade. Both accepted Jesus on the same evening and were baptized in the same warm, enveloping lake. But in spite of how warm and inviting the water was, Jake initially found the experience a little embarrassing. When his head went down, his feet went up—and the spectators all had a good laugh about that. When he finally struggled upright again, he found Brenda's sweet, understanding smile unforgettable. From the moment he dried off, they were inseparable—except when their faith said they should be.

---

**Cyclothymia**

Intermittent or continuous mood swings between mild depression and hypomania (elation or "hyper" emotional state) for two or more years.

A. For at least two years (one year in children and adolescents), there are numerous periods of hypomanic symptoms and numerous periods of minor depression.

B. During the above two years (one year in children and adolescents) the person has not been without the symptoms in A for more than two months at a time.

C. No major depressive episodes.

D. The symptoms cause clinically significant distress or impairment in social, occupational, or other important areas of functioning.

E. The symptoms are not caused by the taking of any chemical substance.

They got married right out of college. Jake had studied to be a criminologist and after graduation got an investigator's job with an insurance company. Brenda settled in to taking care of the home and having their three children—two boys and a girl. In her spare time, which lengthened as the children grew older, Brenda wrote Christian children's books. Even though it was a tough market to crack, she did it with relative ease. And although her books have not become best sellers, she takes satisfaction from knowing they are making a difference in people's lives.

Her children, now eight, six, and five, are all doing well in school. Before they even started kindergarten, they were playing educational games on the household computer. Because of that head start in reading and math, they rarely had trouble learning. And when they did, it was normally just a misunderstanding that could be easily cleared up.

Jake likes his work, and although he can't talk about all aspects of it, he is never at a loss for interesting stories to tell. Some nights they lie in bed after the news and Jake will start talking about this case and that, what he's learned about human nature, or how he's changed his mind about something. And sometimes a comment Brenda makes will give him a helpful new perspective. One of her insights actually enabled Jake to break a case and saved the company several hundred thousand dollars.

Jake and Brenda love each other. While there may be rocky times ahead, the rapids their marriage has negotiated so far have been pretty mild.

When she first came to see Dr. Frank Minirth, things could not have been going better for Brenda. And she knew it.

That's why she couldn't understand her frequent bouts of depression. They came about once every other month and at the strangest times, when the last thing she ought to be is depressed. For example, her daughter, Hannah, the six year old, received an award for a first-grade science project that she had done all by herself—growing a lima bean plant from scratch. A mother should have been beaming with pride as Hannah rose to receive the award, but Brenda wasn't. An annoying under-current of dissatisfaction cut off all emotional sunlight. For several weeks she was on edge, and it was all she could do to keep her anger in check.

But depression is not the only emotion that seems to come out of the blue. There are times when Brenda feels wonderfully happy and alive—elated even. This was never considered a problem; it often seemed to her that the Lord was rewarding her during these times—just giving her a time of excitement and happiness, of contentment and near euphoria.

Nothing special was happening in her life to produce this sense of happiness, but she certainly never begrudged its coming. Since it was such a welcome visitor, she never plotted the frequency; and since it lasted only a week or so, she never thought about it being something abnormal. It was just neat. Of course, there was nothing neat about getting the credit card bills after one of those irresponsible shopping sprees, nor did she get much joy from Jake's groans when he tried to pay them off. But she tried not to think about that. Those difficulties were just part of the price she paid for having that ballooning rush of good feelings and activity.

Then her grandmother died and she woke the day of the funeral with that sense of elation. "Neat" suddenly became dreadful. Brenda found herself singing in the shower and literally dancing around the room as she donned her black mourning dress. Her sense of guilt and propriety ringing all sorts of alarms, she tried to bring herself down. Granny Anna was one of her favorite people. Growing up she had spent wonderful weekends, and now and then a full week, on her apple farm. They would spend warm summer evenings baking apple pies and grinding cider and talking. It was Granny Anna who prayed her into God's kingdom and it was Granny Anna who shepherded her through her difficult teenage years. She owed this woman a lot, and she had every intention of honoring her memory in a sober, respectful, thoughtful manner—and here she was doing a jig while pouring milk into her kids' cereal. And giggling like a schoolgirl when Jeff, her eight year old, came downstairs with his shirt buttoned all wrong.

Although Brenda certainly was not experiencing it at the time, there can be a dark side to hypomania. The sufferer can also be dissatisfied, impatient, and if his or her ideas meet with opposition or those limitless possibilities are thwarted, he or she can become irritable, and even have outbursts of rage. And all this can last four or five days, several weeks, or even longer. Fortunately, Brenda experienced very few bouts of irritability, although there were times during her hypomanic episodes when she got very irritated at how slow people and events were moving around her.

Cyclothymia has a genetic cause. However, the condition can be aggravated by stress and other external forces. As with Warren, we will explore this more thoroughly with Brenda when we get to the steps to wellness.

What about you? Do you see yourself in Brenda? Take the test that follows to see if you should talk to a professional.

(Circle T for true or F for false.)

T  F  I have had mild depressions two or more times in the past two years. (Some cyclothymic individuals have them annually or less, others have them weekly or more.)

T  F  I have had "hyper" periods of elation two or more times in the past two years (again, they can be annually or less, or weekly or more).

T  F  I have one (or more) genetic relatives who has had a major depression or some other form of mood disorder.

T  F  I use prescription and/or illegal drugs and/or alcohol to bring me down when I'm hyper or to lift me up when I'm low.

T  F  During my hyper states, I tend to talk faster and/or dominate the conversation.

T  F  During my hyper states, I tend to become more impulsive (e.g., spending more, flirting more, or other impulsive decisions).

T  F  During my hyper states, I tend to get very little sleep for several nights in a row.

T  F  I have recurrent depressive states during which I may feel tired and sad, but I manage to keep functioning at home, work, and/or school.

T  F  I have had some problems at work, even though I am usually a very hard worker, because of my mood swings.

T  F    I have had relationships that went well when I was "normal" but then developed some problems because of my mood swings.

If you circled five or more Ts, you may be cyclothymic.

## BIPOLAR II

Bipolar II is a bipolar spectrum disorder where the two poles are major depression and hypomania and, as with cyclothymia, there is generally no discernible external cause for either.

In Chapter 1 we met Wendy and her husband, Peter. Further discussion with Wendy confirmed that she suffered from bipolar II. As such, her depressions are severe (major depressions), and every bit as painful and disruptive as Melinda's, whom we met in Chapter 2. And Wendy's highs, her episodes of hypomania, are more pronounced than Brenda's.

---

### Bipolar II

A bipolar spectrum disorder where the two poles are major depression and hypomania.

Anyone who has had one or more major depressions and one or more hypomanic episodes (but never fully manic) probably has the genetic, lifelong disorder known as bipolar II.

A. Presence (or history) of one or more major depressive episodes.

B. Presence (or history) of one of more hypomanic episodes.

C. There has never been a manic episode.

---

D. The symptoms cause clinically significant distress of impairment in social, occupational, or other important areas of functioning.

As with cyclothymia, these moods and mood swings seemingly come out of nowhere. Suddenly, there's a major depression that may last for days, weeks, or months, then just as suddenly a "high" that lasts four or more days (or even weeks)—neither bearing any relationship to the circumstances of the sufferer's life at the time. The lows and highs bring emotional pain and disrupt both the sufferer's life and the lives of those around him or her. But even for a disorder that causes as much disruption as this one does, there is real hope. And as with the other people we've met, you will see the process Wendy goes through to achieve wellness.

What about you? Do you see yourself in Wendy? Take the test that follows to see if you should talk to a professional. (Circle T for true or F for false.)

T  F   I have had at least one major depression (see major depression and diagnostic test in previous chapter).

T  F   I have had at least one hypomanic episode lasting four or more days during which I never lost touch with reality, but I made some grandiose and impulsive decisions that got me into embarrassing trouble (like spending way too much, having an impulsive sexual affair, or making unwise business decisions, etc.).

T  F   During my depression(s), I wished I could die and/or I had difficulty functioning at my normal routine for two or more weeks.

T   F   During my hypomanic episode(s), I was told that I talked too fast or too much, dominating conversations.

T   F   During my hypomanic episode(s), I slept little or not at all for four or more nights in a row.

T   F   During my hypomanic episode(s), I was hyperactive, restless, and could not remain still. I could not have sat quietly and watched a two-hour movie during that time.

T   F   During my hypomanic episode(s), I became more irritable with those who disagreed with me or hassled me.

T   F   During my hypomanic episode(s), I had racing thoughts and ideas. I could not turn my mind off to rest.

T   F   During my hypomanic episode(s), I felt wiser or better than others, but not to the point of becoming grossly delusional (I didn't think I was Jesus, or Mother Teresa, or a new prophet discovering the "key to the universe," for example).

T   F   I have one (or more) genetic relatives who has had a major depression and/or some other mood disorder at some time in their lives.

If you answered five or more of the questions true, you may very well have bipolar II.

Let's take this one step further. Imagine, if you will, that you are an executive of a large company, or perhaps even an elected official who fulfills your responsibility faithfully inside the Washington Beltway. Imagine that you find yourself inexplicably plunged into a deep depression. You seek psychological help, get on antidepressant medication, overcome the depression, and have a sense of victory sweep over you. After several weeks or even months, you are finally able to return to work. Months go by and you begin to forget that you even had the depression. Job and life are moving along as swimmingly as before.

Then, suddenly, you find yourself elated, talking a mile a minute. Ideas are flashing before your eyes like a lightning storm—you feel as if you're the king of the intellectual world. But you become too hyper to function, and you even get to the point where you suddenly proclaim to everyone who will listen that you are God and that you have a plan to solve all the world's troubles—and you believe these grandiose delusions.

What's wrong? You are suffering from bipolar I.

## BIPOLAR I

Although sufferers of bipolar I are normal people who are living their lives like the rest of us—they have families, jobs, go to church, love God—there comes a terrible time when their high, their manic moment, causes severe disruption of their lives, their jobs, or their relationships with family and friends. Their manic episodes may land them in a hospital, or, worse yet, cause them to break through the ceiling of reality into a world of emotional and intellectual fantasy. Here the person he or she normally is becomes an object of ridicule, and perhaps real danger.

### Bipolar I

A bipolar spectrum disorder where the two poles are major depression and mania.

Anyone who has had one or more major depressions and one or more full-blown manic episodes (in which the individual's life was significantly disrupted and which may have included losing touch with reality) probably has the genetic, lifelong disorder known as bipolar I.

Left untreated, the sufferer will return to normal, but not before causing significant disruption to his or her own life and the lives of family and friends. Many (as high as ten percent) will even commit suicide, often in a state of psychotic confusion.

What about you? Do you see yourself in this discussion of bipolar I? Take the test that follows to see if you should talk to a professional. (Circle T for true or F for false.)

T  F  *I have had at least one major depression (see major depression and diagnostic test in previous chapter).

T  F  *I have had at least one "hyper" period lasting four or more days during which I actually lost touch with reality, with one or more grandiose or paranoid delusions (e.g., believed my phone was bugged, God told me to write a whole book tonight explaining the meaning of life, someone is poisoning my food, strangers were talking about me behind my back, satellites are reading my mind, etc.), and/or I heard "voices" inside my head that were clearly audible. (Twenty percent of bipolar I's lose touch with reality like this).

T  F  During my depression(s), I wished I could die and/or I had difficulty functioning at my normal routine for two or more weeks.

T  F     During my manic episode(s), I was told that I talked too fast or too much, and dominated conversations.

T  F     During my manic episode(s), I slept little or not at all for four or more nights in a row.

T  F     During my manic episode(s), I was hyperactive, restless, and could not remain still. I could not have sat quietly and watched a two-hour movie during that time.

T  F     During my manic episode(s), I became very irritable with those who dared to disagree with me or hassled me.

T  F     During my manic episode(s), I had racing thoughts and ideas. I could not turn my mind off to rest.

T  F     *During my manic episode(s), I became so "hyper" that I could no longer function adequately at work or in financial decisions or in my relationships. (Some bipolar I's pull off their clothes and run down Main Street naked or exhibit other bizarre behaviors that are way out of character for that person. Others waste life savings in one day on a foolish spending spree.)

T  F     I have one (or more) genetic relatives who has had a major depression and/or they had another mood disorder at some time in their lives.

If you answered five or more of the questions true, and they include at least two of those marked with an asterisk (*), then you may very well have bipolar I. Again, with therapy, education, and proper lifelong medication, you can probably live a very normal (or close to normal) life.

In later chapters we will work with you through a process that should bring your life back into emotional balance. But before we do, there are two things to consider. If your scores are significantly higher on any of the self-tests, seek qualified psychiatric help immediately. And, if you are seriously considering suicide, seek help immediately then go directly to Chapter 5, read what we have for you there. You are too precious to us and to God to do anything else.

Now that we have described the various moods and mood swings and helped you identify where you fit among them, let's take a look at how moods and mood swings affect your life. If there is still a part of you that does not want to expend the energy to deal with them, we hope that part of you will evaporate after reading this next chapter.

# 4 HOW MOODS AND MOOD SWINGS AFFECT YOUR LIFE

If nothing could be done about moods and mood swings, it might make perfect sense for sufferers to intellectually dismiss the effects moods have on their lives. Ignoring our moods usually results in severe consequences for us and those we love.

But something can be done.

Doing something means change, however, and change, for all of us, is difficult. This chapter will present a host of effects that moods and mood swings have on every human being. It may be that you will see a variety of harmful mood swings active in your own life. But even if you see only a few, a few is far too many and far too destructive. Our hope, of course, is that your reluctance to make the necessary changes to master your moods will fade.

So let's take a look at what those effects are. The first to consider is that moods corrupt our focus and the view others have of us.

Scripture is full of references that call us to live for others, to spread the gospel (the good news about God) to others, to always live our lives conscious of our witness. Our focus, whenever possible, should be outward, as we minister to the people around us. But when we find ourselves struggling with a mood—depression, elation, irritability, whatever—suddenly our focus is on ourselves.

That was certainly true of Melinda. The moment she began her slide into depression, all her energy was turned to getting through the day—making sure her own needs were met. Even her children's need for bag lunches, her husband's need for companionship, the house's need to be cleaned, all took second place to Melinda's need for self-preservation. Now, that's not to say that she could wake up one morning and just decide to refocus on those around her. Quite the contrary, at this point in her life she has very little control over her focus.

That's the point. It's as if Melinda were peering through a pair of binoculars all her life, a pair she had firmly in hand and focused on all those things outside. Then suddenly, just as a child might, her moods grabbed the binoculars and focused them somewhere else. Now she is focused where her depression wants, and she is hard pressed to do anything about it.

This leads to the next destructive effect moods have on sufferers: they make the sufferer feel that he or she is inherently emotionally weak. Slaves always felt that way, even though slaves were often the strongest people around. Even though they toiled long, hard hours doing backbreaking work, they still felt impotent. That weakness they saw as a weakness of soul. They were subjugated, forced to do things they did not want to do, and they felt weak because they could not safely rebel.

The same is true for the sufferer and his or her emotions. Dr. Meier could see Melinda's weakness the instant she stepped into the room. She moved without purpose, without interest, as if nothing she did mattered and if she actually did want to do something meaningful, she would be prevented. Weakness. And weakness strips us of self-respect. People who are respected have strength, have the ability to make things happen, and can stand up for themselves even against the strongest enemy.

Not Melinda, particularly in her own eyes. She was not dealing with an emotional weakness, but a weakness of self. That's why her jokes at the beginning of her session with Paul were self-demeaning—she called herself a stick-in-the-mud and joked that her sister wanted to be just like her, implying, of course, that her sister did not. No one else did either.

How is your self-respect when you think about your slavery to your moods? Do you feel you are less because you can't erase your moods?

Just as the sufferer's sense of reality about herself is corrupted, so is the sufferer's view of reality as a whole. For the world takes on a different look depending on your mood. For Brenda, who suffers from cyclothymia, when she's normal the kids are bright and cheerful, their little idiosyncrasies are endearing, their arguments no big deal. Reality for her is pretty good. Nothing there to give her pause, she can sail right through it all—God has prepared her for all of it, and she's just clicking off the situations encountered like a second hand sweeping around the clock face.

But when her cyclothymia swings her into a depression, Brenda's reality turns to chaos. The kids are impossible and need psychiatric help. If there's a problem in her writing, it's the problem that will force her to give up and mail back her advance. Life becomes one crisis after another. And she is right in the middle of them.

This is the most damaging of the reality shifts: she is the problem. Brenda knows she's being impatient. She thinks it's her fault things are out of control. Yesterday, when she got up and happily got everyone off to wherever they were going, she was the solution. Today, she thinks the chaos is something she herself has caused. This reality shift is by far the most destructive because she thinks, erroneously, that she is the problem, and she has no idea how to correct it. So not only must she deal with the destruction in her wake, but she must deal with not knowing how to deal with herself. And this is the deepest kind of frustration.

So moods and mood swings alter the reality of how we and others see us. That in itself is a reason to work to eliminate them from your life. But there's more.

## MOODS AND MOOD SWINGS ARE DISRUPTIVE

Moods and mood swings disrupt the rhythm of the sufferer's life.

We live our lives at a certain energy level, and a certain level of activity. When Brenda rose in the morning, she knew that she could shower, get the kids up, get their lunches made, get Jake off to work, get the first load of clothes in the washer, and be at the word processor banging out a children's book by ten o'clock. And, give or take a phone call or two, there she was. She planned on it. When she took a writing assignment, she used these time gauges to estimate when she would turn in the manuscript.

But when a bad mood hit, the rhythm disintegrated. Now it was all she could do to get up in the morning. The shower took a lot longer—when she is feeling down, nothing soothes her more than warm water running all over her. Dealing with the kids took longer too. Arguments popped like popcorn, making every hiccup in the morning routine a major disruption. And, of course, Brenda was late getting downstairs to prepare breakfast and the lunches. And getting Jake off. After all, he can take care of himself. If he wants that special coffee so he can spill it all over his clean white shirt on the way to work—well, he can make it himself.

Life's rhythm, the rhythm we count on to tell us all is well and moving smoothly, is grossly out of kilter when we are in the throes of a bad mood swing, which means that we're instantly left with the impression that all is not well. Another source of stress.

And as those moods and mood swings disrupt our lives, they are also disrupting our relationships.

Relationships are formed largely on what we expect from ourselves and other people. If we expect the other person to be understanding, we're more open with our feelings. If we expect a sarcastic bite now and again, we're less open. So when we have a relationship with a sufferer, and suddenly the sufferer is not who he or she was yesterday, then something's wrong and we pull back.

That's what it was like for Wendy. Because she loved history and was enthusiastic about it, she infected several students with that same enthusiasm. And they loved and respected her for it. These students often came around after class to talk with her about that day's lesson. Like any teacher would, she began looking forward to these sessions. But when Wendy became Ms. Chimp, those same students suddenly were embarrassed to be around her. She was no longer the same thoughtful, enthusiastic teacher; now she was a very strange woman—a nut case.

For this and other reasons, the sufferer is also often seen as emotionally weak and unstable. This can be particularly troubling to the Christian. As believers, we work hard to present a respectable image, one that others can turn to in hours of need, one that reflects the steadfastness of Jesus. But moods change all that, and our image of stability can be severely tarnished.

And a large part of a reputation for unsteadiness rests in the fact that those who suffer from moods and mood swings often do things they have to undo later.

Moods, by their very nature, cause us to do things we would not normally do. Wendy would never have thrown those homework papers across the room normally. But when she did, a couple of the papers ripped almost in half. Later she had to apologize to those students for damaging their work. But that was a minor incident, one easily repaired.

Other incidents could not be repaired at all. Wendy had a dear friend, Ginny. They had gone through much of college together, and it was Wendy who had convinced Ginny to attempt teaching. She had been there for Ginny during the naturally difficult time of her fifth year—her student teaching and preparation to earn her credentials. They had been fortunate to get jobs in the same town and were able to continue their friendship. But teaching did not come as easily to Ginny as it seemed to for Wendy. A number of times Wendy had to snatch Ginny back from giving up and resigning.

One time, when Ginny got depressed again, she gave Wendy a call. But this time Wendy was having one of her highs—she was Ms. Chimp. After only a few minutes on the phone, a very disturbed Ginny hung up. Unable to get a serious answer or thought or word of encouragement out of Wendy, she placed the phone back on the receiver. The next day she resigned. A few days later Ginny returned home, about two thousand miles away, and Wendy never spoke to her again.

Like Wendy, Brenda is forever doing repair work after one of her moods, particularly with Jake. Every time she misses making his coffee the way he likes it, she is flying in the face of one of their cherished "I love you" things. He gets up at least ten minutes before she does to prepare her special coffee, a vanilla nut blend she especially likes. So when she's feeling down, Brenda gets her coffee, but Jake doesn't get his. But even more important, she has to make sure the kids have no ill effects from her impatience. Often after a mood, she will spend as much time as possible with them.

For someone who experiences moods and mood swings, repair work is a matter of course. But a person learns quickly:

although you can repair, you can never erase. Brenda knows her kids will always remember those impatient mornings. Mommy will have always been a good mommy, except . . .

Not only must relational repair work be done, the decisions the sufferer makes while in a mood are always suspect.

## DIMINISHED CAPACITY FOR DECISION-MAKING

When Brenda is in a mood, what do you think her decisions are like? When she's on a high, her decisions are from the hip; they have an element of irresponsibility about them. She makes decisions without considering the downside too seriously. Melinda, who is suffering from major depression, makes overly cautious decisions, preoccupied with the dark side of whatever the decision concerns. Melinda does not shop for clothes too often anymore. She doesn't see the point. But when her husband insisted she get a new dress for a business function, she chose black. It was for the company Christmas party. The problem, of course, is that sometimes decisions *have* to be made. There was no way Melinda was going to beg off getting a new outfit. Don was insistent—it was his way of propelling her out of the house. So a decision was inevitable.

Brenda, too, finds that when she's writing a story during one of her moods, the characters tend to reveal their darker sides—little rabbits, instead of enjoying the aroma of beautiful flowers, will rip them to shreds and dance upon the torn petals.

Sometimes the decisions are a little more far reaching. And when we're in our moods, sometimes we really want to make them. "I'll show that miserable little so-and-so how not to treat me." Have you ever made a decision you've later regretted because you made it in a mood?

So, because the impact of our moods can be so destructive, the sufferer needs to be constantly on guard. Rather than being emotionally free—or as emotionally free as others—those who suffer from moods and mood swings are constantly testing their emotions to see if they are in the beginning stages of a mood. Brenda finds herself watching for the onset of depression all the time. Every negative feeling causes her to stop and examine it. And when she does, even her normal times take on a hesitancy and a preoccupation that removes her a little from life's excitement and spontaneity.

Is that true for you? Being in constant control of an emotional filter can be taxing. But there's another thing that can be just as taxing, and a whole lot trickier for the sufferer: scheduling one-time important events.

We also say it this way: How do you schedule a picnic during a midwestern summer, when it just might rain?

What if you have to go in for a parent/teacher conference when you are really depressed? Or if your family is considering adoption and the interview, a time when you want to appear particularly cheerful and able to cope, comes on one of *those* days? Let's list a few others. How about your job review, or the first-time meeting with your boss's boss? Or if you find yourself accused of something you just didn't do and need to defend yourself? We're sure you can come up with a few more, maybe even a couple you have experienced personally. Life is full of these moments when we have to be at our best, and suddenly, through what appears to be no fault of our own, we're not.

But the greatest, and probably the most destructive disruption of all, is the fact that 70 percent of those suffering from moderate to severe moods or mood swings are alcoholics and/or drug abusers. This is not to suggest that you are, but because of the tension produced by moods and mood swings, those suffering from them often medicate themselves with alcohol and/or illegal drugs. Assuming you're not an abuser, your moods or mood swings, if left unchecked, can only get worse.

This, in turn, increases the likelihood that you may become a substance abuser in the future. Not a pleasant outlook. And, just as depression often leads to alcoholism, alcoholism also leads to depression, because alcohol depletes serotonin from the brain, and alcoholism also destroys relationships.

We have seen how moods and mood swings alter your view of reality and cause your life to be disrupted in several different ways, but one of the more frustrating things moods and mood swings do to the sufferer is to cause legitimate feelings to go unacknowledged.

## Loss of Legitimate Feelings

How do you think Wendy responds when something wonderful happens to her? Well, something wonderful did happen to her. As a budding historian, she submitted an article about the Revolutionary War to a prestigious journal. A couple of months passed and she had all but forgotten it. Then during her lunch break at school, she received a letter telling her the article had been accepted for publication. The instant she read the words her heart began feeling like a helium balloon—her pulse quickened and her blood started to pump as if she had been injected with adrenaline. Wendy was sure she was about to become Ms. Chimp. Since that was one side of her she definitely did not want to be revealed, especially on an occasion like this, she quickly excused herself and spent the rest of the day, except for her two afternoon classes, huddled alone in an obscure office off the women's gym—unable to share her good news with anyone.

Wendy was simply feeling a healthy rush of excitement. But when you suffer from moods, not only do you suppress or fight your legitimate feelings, you begin to doubt them as well. After all, if one set of feelings can come at us out of thin air, then others can too.

Brenda finds depressions settling in like ducks settling on a lake—randomly and without apparent provocation. What if she suddenly finds herself getting irritable, or even angry? What if these feelings come and stay awhile? Worse yet, what if they just won't go away? What might she think? She would chalk the feeling up to another mood and just bear it. In fact, though, she could be picking up some signals from her husband that were causing this anger. Maybe he is reacting to her differently—not grossly so, but in small ways. Little looks of dissatisfaction, little comments that demean her, little acts that dismiss her as a person. These things can quickly add up, and in a sensitive person they can produce strong and legitimate feelings. So instead of confronting the issues that produce these feelings, something that healthy people do, the feelings are buried in the graveyard of "it's just a mood." And only later, when they can't be buried any longer, they rise to the surface to take their destructive toll on a relationship.

Just as sufferers begin to suppress, fight, and doubt their legitimate feelings, the people around them also dismiss the sufferer's legitimate feelings.

Depression can lead to angry outbursts. Brenda saw this anger in herself with the kids, and with Jake. But sometimes her anger is not the result of the mood, but rather the result of someone close to her overstepping a recognized boundary. Perhaps her husband has treated her shabbily, or her children have been blatantly disobedient, or any number of other possibilities. So Brenda gets legitimately angry. But instead of respecting her expression of anger, the kids and Jake respond by saying, "Well, aren't we in a mood again." Or, "Mom's just in another one of those moods." The sufferer's legitimate emotions are totally dismissed.

So far we have discussed some pretty destructive things moods and mood swings do to the sufferer, but they pale when compared to this last one: withdrawing from God.

## God Becomes an Outsider

If there is a reason to start working to eliminate your moods and/or mood swings, this is it. As human beings beset by the devil, the world, and our own sinful flesh, the last thing in the world we need is one more reason to push God away. And moods give it to us.

Because we are slaves to our moods, our prayers to be delivered from them in all likelihood have gone unanswered. We see bad things happening to us because of our moods, things that, in our eyes at least, God could not possibly want. We see our witness tarnished, our effectiveness in whatever job God has given us diminished, our relationships often pushed to the breaking point. We see all this going on and God never seems to intervene. In fact, He even appears not to care. And if He does not care about this element of our lives, what else is He leaving up to chance? Instead of a guiding light in our lives, God is relegated to a good-to-have-around, ineffective uncle instead of a loving Father.

Well, to answer that, we would like to hope that God has brought you to this book, and we also hope you are sincere about making God the center of your life again.

Your moods may have done other things to you that we've missed. If so, make your own list. Then the reason to begin working on mastering your moods is even greater.

In the next chapter, we are going to address the issue of suicide. Of course, whether you have ever contemplated suicide or not, we urge you to read it. Even if it is not an issue for you now, reading these words may help keep it from becoming one.

# 5

# BATTLING THE TEMPTATION TO END IT ALL

One of the worst things moods can do, particularly those involving depression, is to cause the sufferers to contemplate suicide—either while experiencing the depression, or as relief from the roller coaster of their mood swings. Since suicide is such a destructive—and permanent—reaction to something as treatable as moods, it is important that we address this topic.

At some point in their lives most people will have at least a fleeting thought about suicide. Even young children sometimes threaten suicide to manipulate parents. We know a teenager who got a very large zit on his nose the day of the senior prom and felt suicide was the only alternative. Fortunately, he found that Clearasil was another. Of course, we're injecting a little humor in a very serious subject, for not only does suicide have a certain appeal to solving skin problems, it also gives the potential victim what appears to be an easy ticket out of the pain and the rat race we all find ourselves in from time to time.

But we believe the main reason perfectly well-balanced people can at times contemplate suicide is that it plays very nicely into Satan's hands. He certainly wants us to reject the life God has planned for us, and if a person is unsaved, Satan wants them to die that way. So it's likely he or his minions will suggest it to most folks sometime during his evil ministry toward them.

If you have considered suicide as an option sometime in the past, you're not alone. Even if your consideration of this step is serious, it's quite logical to want to end your depression, to somehow salve the pain for the last time. But though the thoughts seem logical, that does not mean they are appropriate and valuable. They aren't. Depression is curable. And with a little work, and perhaps a little medicine, the ticket off the roller coaster is all but in your hand right now.

## ARE YOU AT RISK?

But for some that knowledge alone is not enough, and they are still at risk for a suicide attempt. Are you at risk? Only you as an individual really know, but the following points are ones that are important in making that determination.

### TALKING ABOUT IT

You have talked about committing suicide with a friend or loved one. If someone feels suicidal, sharing those feelings with a friend makes it less likely to happen. And yet most of those who actually do attempt this terrible act have mentioned their intentions to someone close to them. Of course, talking about it is like the tip of an iceberg. The actual consideration of it, the time your brain spends thinking about it, is much greater and hidden below the surface when compared to the few minutes spent voicing the issue. For that reason, if you have gotten to the point where you have broached the subject with someone, then there is a problem.

### THINKING ABOUT IT

You have found yourself in reverie thinking about it. If you have ever found yourself daydreaming about how wonderful it might be to leave this life and somehow float unperturbed through a wonderfully nurturing eternity, then please share that with someone who loves you. If you have mused for a long period of time, or for several shorter bursts, about suddenly leaving this war we call life and found yourself loving, even looking forward to the idea—if the idea of death is far better than any hope you might have for the future—then you need to seek professional help.

## CHOOSING A METHOD

Suicide requires a method, some way to take your life. If you have found yourself trying to choose one, and even weighing the pros and cons of each method—availability, how you will be found, if it will hurt, etc.—then you are closer to it than you might think. Inpatient, or at least outpatient, treatment is often recommended to get past this serious risk.

## COMPOSING A SUICIDE NOTE

If you have composed a suicide note either in your head or on paper, you are at risk. Only 10 to 15 percent of suicide victims leave a note, but that does not make suicide any less profound a statement. The last thing a sufferer may want is for his suicide to be misinterpreted, so he composes a message. Have you written one? Have you thought in general terms what such a note might say? Have you gone through the trouble of choosing just the right words? If you have, inpatient treatment is recommended until you are "over the hump."

## GAUGING THE REACTION OF OTHERS

If you have gone through the list of your loved ones and friends and wondered how each would react, this may signal danger. Those contemplating taking their own lives usually do not want the act to be ignored. They want to believe (and, of course, they're right) that those around them will have a profound reaction. Those actually contemplating suicide will go through a pretty extensive list of those close to them and try to determine, based on their current relationship, how that person will react. If you have come up with a number who just won't care, or who will now be forced to take notice of you where before they didn't, then it's time to seek real help right away.

## ATTEMPTED SUICIDE

If you have actually attempted suicide and failed, and are truly disappointed for the failure, you need treatment. We helped a young lady who took a whole prescription of what she thought were powerful sedatives, but which, in fact, were not. When she awoke the next morning she had a headache but little else. She was also terribly disappointed, and within twenty-four hours she tried again. Fortunately, she failed a second time. This attempt was discovered and caring friends coaxed her into coming to our clinic. If you have attempted suicide and you feel overwhelmingly disappointed at the failure, seek help today. Ten percent of those who survive a suicide attempt end up actually killing themselves some time later.

If any of these descriptions sound like what you are currently going through, before you attempt such a permanent and destructive non-solution to your problems, keep reading.

How is it that moods, which come and go, can cause such a permanent response?

## MOODS ALTER THE SENSE OF REALITY

When people are in a depressed mood, they may have an altered sense of reality. Even though they have been in and out of these moods many times, they feel that while they are in one, it's a permanent condition. If you are severely depressed, you think you will never be happy again. If you are irritable, you think you will never be calm again. If you are on a manic high, like Wendy, you think you will never come down again. So when you're in a mood, it's quite easy to believe that the mood (and how you perceive the world while in it) is exactly how things are. Reality, however, is somewhere else altogether.

The first thing to realize is that moods are just that—moods—and they will pass. We believe nearly every suicide throughout history could have been prevented if the victim had seen the truth rather than the lies misperceived by the moods and by the forces of evil.

Sometimes it is not the moods themselves but the mood swings that are really getting to you. Rather than the altered sense of reality, it is the roller coaster of mood swings that is driving you toward the cliff. It's waking up in the morning and realizing you are going to be someone else that day, that you're going to hurt people, or drive your family that much farther away. If that's where you are, then may we give you hope. Within these pages is a formula that has helped thousands of people get off the treadmill of mood swings, principles that have allowed them to master their moods.

You do not have to stop breathing to achieve relief. Quite the contrary, taking those days one at a time, and taking things as they come with courage, will deliver you from whatever those mood swings bring. It may even take the courage and humility to admit that you have a genetic mood disorder and are willing to take lifelong medication to correct it.

And as Christians, we must further consider the moral and ethical implications of suicide.

## ETHICS AND SUICIDE

Suicide is self-murder. The Ten Commandments clearly prohibit murder. But you know that already, so if you're thinking about suicide, you have already discounted that. Yet there are other biblical passages to ponder.

Three thousand years ago, King David, who survived his own suicidal mood swings, wrote Psalm 139, which tells us about the moment we were created. "For you created my inmost being; / you knit me together in my mother's womb. / I praise you because I am fearfully and wonderfully made; / your works are wonderful" (vv. 13–14 NIV). David came to the realization that we are each a wonderful work of God, and God does not make mistakes.

Granted, at this particular moment, you may not feel you are so wonderfully made, but God says differently. In fact, He loves you so much, He nailed His Son to a cross for you. But that's not where it stops. He tells us in Romans 8:32, "He who did not spare his own Son, but gave him up for us all—how will he not also, along with him, graciously give us all things?" (NIV). Again, it may not seem that you are getting "all things" now (or some of the things you're getting, you wish He would keep to Himself), but that does not change the fact that He has an abundant life for you—and all you have to do is live it.

The other thing to realize is that even deeply spiritual people can wish for and even pray for death. King David, who once said under the inspiration of the Holy Spirit that his heart panted after God as a deer after a waterbrook, knew what it was like to feel terribly depressed. In Psalm 13, he describes it like this:

How long, O LORD? Will you forget me forever?
How long will you hide your face from me?
How long must I wrestle with my thoughts
and every day have sorrow in my heart? (vv. 1–2 NIV)

Is that how you feel right now? As if the Lord has deserted you, left you to fend for yourself in an extremely hostile world?

Those negative feelings passed for David and were replaced by these feelings:

> I love you, O LORD, my strength.
> The LORD is my rock, my fortress and my deliverer;
> my God is my rock, in whom I take refuge.
> He is my shield and the horn of my salvation, my stronghold.
> (Psalm 18:1–2 NIV)

These will hopefully be your words soon.

## THE EFFECTS OF SUICIDE ON THE SURVIVORS

If you are still thinking seriously about ending it all, consider what your act will do to those you leave behind.

You may think that you will just vanish off the face of the earth, or that those left behind won't miss you one bit. Yet it is quite natural for those who have lost a loved one or friend to suicide to go through some pretty profound emotional trauma. We would like to list some of the effects for you now.

### STIGMA

Look at how you feel about someone whose child or spouse committed suicide—someone you know, or perhaps a celebrity. Don't you wonder if they may have done something to the victim to "force" him into making such a drastic and irreversible choice? Or don't you sometimes wonder why they didn't see it coming? Didn't he (or she) say anything? Suicide creates false guilt in the survivors, and they may feel branded with a stigma. The person who commits suicide is responsible for his own choice, even though biochemical mood swings heavily influenced that decision in most cases. Many bipolar sufferers may die of suicide, and these are needless deaths that this book's advice could help prevent. We pray it will save the lives of thousands.

## PAIN AND ANGER

Have you ever experienced the unexpected death of someone close—perhaps in a traffic accident or a weather-related catastrophe like a flood or hurricane? Relive that sense of pain, of helplessness, then of anger—anger at the person, anger at God, anger at yourself. Suicide makes all the pain and anger that much more pronounced. Suicide is usually a profoundly premeditated act. It is seldom casual. So someone close to the victim, a parent or sibling, or a close friend, can legitimately get angry at the victim. "How could he have done that to me, to his kids, to those who love him?" "How could she deprive us in this way? We loved her, wanted the best for her, and she did this!" And a lot of the anger is to cover the deep pain that comes from being rejected—for even though there are arguments against it, suicide can be seen as the ultimate rejection of your love for that person.

But there's more—the pain of suddenly being thrust into a terribly hollow helplessness. The desire to help when you no longer can, the desire to make someone happy or bring meaning to a life. And now there's no longer a way. Just the pain of loss. The victim was connected to you—by memories, responsibilities, a hope for the future—and suddenly all those threads are ripped out of the survivors, like a thousand hooks tearing at their emotional flesh. The pain can be quite profound.

## NO CHANCE TO SAY GOOD-BYE

Good-byes are important. It gives us a chance to sum things up, express our love, let the person know that she was and will continue to be important. It gives those who are saying farewell the chance to say what is on their hearts, make that final connection, help the person move on to whatever's next—we hope heaven. But the suicide victim denies this final moment to those close to him. And by denying them this, he leaves some very profound feelings in limbo.

## PHYSICAL ILLNESS

Those close to a suicide victim experience worsening health. Those who suffer from diabetes or high blood pressure will usually see both worsen considerably, and even if hypertension is not a problem before, it may become a problem afterward. For the survivors now have even more to worry about—their own health and the health of others who survived. After all, if one member of the family chooses suicide, why not another? And if they missed the telltale signs in that family member, maybe they will miss those same signs in someone else. The tension can quickly cause a lowered resistance to physical illness.

## A DAY OF INFAMY

The day you commit suicide will become a day of infamy. No matter what the date the suicide is committed, it will never be forgotten. It will be relived over and over again. Not only the day, but the moment the suicide was discovered. Just as no one forgets what they were doing when they heard President Kennedy was shot, no one in your family will forget the moment they found your body. "I woke up and it was like every other day. He said good-bye and went off to work and the next thing I knew I was getting a call—he had killed himself. April fifteenth. Every April fifteenth I wake up with this dread in my heart. Why couldn't I have seen it coming?"

## LACK OF SUPPORT

Less support comes to the survivors of a suicide. The stigma of suicide attaches to the survivors and keeps them from getting the kind of support other survivors of a loved one's sudden death get. For other survivors, there are support groups. People from church call and express their sympathies, friends stand by them and call frequently just to talk. But the stigma of suicide prevents much of that. Often people just don't know what to say to the survivors. If a friend's spouse dies of cancer, we can express sympathy freely. But when a person commits suicide, what do you say? Granted, you can say the same thing, but there is another element here. The person took his or her life voluntarily, and that adds a dimension that somehow needs to be expressed. "He was such a neat guy . . ." just doesn't say it all. "I'm sorry he killed himself" doesn't cut it, either. So, instead of getting tongue-tied about it, people just say nothing and often give no support at all.

## INCREASED TRAUMA TO THE FAMILY

Suicides happen in families, even very nice families. Think of yours. Do you wish the best for them? Do you want them, as a support unit, to remain healthy and vital? Then don't commit suicide. The shock waves that rock a family unit after a suicide run deep. For instance, 70 percent of the parents of teen suicides, spouses bound by love and commitment, end their marriages in divorce. And because of the social stigma associated with suicide, most families move afterward, forcing siblings into forming new friendships and support structures. And now, each one of those new relationships starts under an anxious cloud — will this person kill himself too?

## VALUES QUESTIONED

A suicide causes those left behind to question their values. Those closest to the suicide victim are usually from the same social, economic, spiritual, and emotional backgrounds. Now someone has rejected those values in the firmest of terms. This notion is never stronger than if one of those values is Christianity. If the suicide victim is known to be a Christian, it is hard not to believe that God has in some way failed His child—and if He can fail that child, He can fail me. This sends real tremors through the survivors' faith. Do you want to be responsible for damaging the faith of a loved one? We would hope not.

## LOSS OF TRUST

Suicide creates a loss of trust in the survivors' own feelings and sense of worth. What if your sibling has once thought about suicide—a thought we've said is quite common—and suddenly you actually do it? How frightened might your brother or sister become? Don't you think they would wonder if one day they might actually wake up and decide life is not worth living? Wouldn't they wonder what feelings led up to your doing it—and wonder if they might not actually be on the same track? The suicide of a loved one dampens everything—turns everything to shades of gray and tinges those things that used to taste sweet with a lingering note of bitterness and failure. Your suicide makes the eventual suicide of your loved ones more likely.

## DELAYED GRIEF

The grief over your death may come in waves, sometimes decades apart. Because of the complexity of the grief process for the survivors of a suicide, the process might be arrested for months, even years, then—perhaps accompanying another tragedy in life—grief from the suicide might come again just as strong, as insistent as a tide. What your suicide will unleash on those close to you is emotionally profound, horribly damaging, and will batter their shores for a long, long time.

## GUILT

And the guilt—oh, the guilt. False guilt in particular—assuming responsibility for someone else's decision.

"We could have done something. I know we could have."

71

"I can't speak ill of the dead, yet I'm so angry. How could I be so angry at him? What kind of person am I?"

"How can I be enjoying life again like this? He's dead and I could have saved him. How could I be happy again?"

"I can't believe I'm glad he's gone. He was such a burden while he was here, but not a big enough burden that I'd want him dead. What kind of person am I?"

"It's been years, yet sometimes I still hear him whistling out there on the porch. I know I did something. I was part of his life and he couldn't stand his life. Till the day I die I will hate myself for what I did to him."

You don't really want to end your life.

That's not what you want. No matter how depressed or weary you might be, you don't really want to end it all. Doesn't that run a distant second to living a fulfilling, abundant life, where every day is a thrilling new adventure, where even the lows are rewarding for the strength they eventually give? That's the kind of life you want. And we can offer that life to you. Keep reading. By the last page, you will be far along the trail leading to a happier life.

# 6

## Your Brain:

### God's Magnificent Creation

In the last chapter we looked at the Psalm that says we are "fearfully and wonderfully made" (139:14). If there is proof that God exists, and that He's a loving, caring God, it is the human brain. Not only is it wonderfully complex—which points to God's own complexity and His creative power—but it also points to His love: the brain is capable of motivating great sacrifice for others, the very definition of love, as well as taking care of the body it serves. Yet because of its great complexity and all the things, both physically and emotionally, it is called upon to do, the brain can become imbalanced—and then *we* become off balance, as well, since our brain is so closely aligned with who we are as individuals.

So, in order to begin dealing with our moods and mood swings, we need to take a little closer look at our brains, and perhaps view them a little differently.

On her first visit, as Melinda sat in Dr. Meier's office discussing her recent desire to do nothing, she related how she, as a person, felt—disinterested in work, or any activity for that matter, even to the point of not wanting to get up in the morning. She did not say, "My brain doesn't want to get up, doesn't want to fix lunches for the kids, or spend meaningful time with my husband." She said *she* did not want to do those things. She was the stick-in-the-mud, not her brain. Yet feelings originate in the brain. Why don't we say our brain is feeling depressed today? Or our brain is frightened? Instead, we say we're feeling depressed, we're feeling nervous, we're feeling confused.

Why? After all, if our hand hurts when we open and close it, we would identify the problem as just that: my hand has a problem. If your toe hurts so much you can't take your morning walk, you would tell the doctor, "My toe hurts." That's the way we look at it. Our hands, our feet, our eyes, our liver, our gallbladder—these things are part of us, yet they aren't actually us. They are separate somehow. We talk about them as external to the real us, existing as tools we use or facilitators we depend on—but separate, able to be removed.

Of course, pain or disease in any body part can be so severe that it takes over our every thought and movement. But even then we have not become our painful extremity or diseased organ; we have become captive to it. Our thoughts, our attitudes, and our emotions are all placed behind the iron curtain of pain or disease, waiting to emerge when the curtain rises to free us.

The opposite can also be true.

Our body—our extremities, our organs, our muscles—can be in excellent shape. They can be the picture of health and vitality, capable of leaping tall buildings in a single bound, or taking on great thinkers in debate, or witnessing to thousands, but we—the real us—can hold our bodies captive. Our fear of failure may keep us from competing, or a sudden rush of depression may keep us from debating or witnessing. Or, as with Melinda, the sudden onset of an emotional low keeps a perfectly healthy body from being "all it can be" in God's kingdom.

That, of course, is what this book will help the reader correct.

So, in spite of our thinking that we are depressed, it may actually be our brain physiology that is depressing us. When we drive people away because we're unsure of who we are from day to day, can we also say it is our brain that is emotionally exhausted, or depressed, or varying emotionally from highs to lows to in-betweens? "We" and our brains are somehow interchangeable, especially if we have a genetic predisposition towards various mood swings.

Our brain, therefore, holds a special place within us. Even though it is a physical organ, weighing about three to four pounds and physically located in the protective confines of our skulls just behind our eyes and forehead, it is quite unique and has a unique identity: it houses who we are. And just as God would want us to take advantage of surgery for a fractured hand, there is every reason to believe He also wants us to seek medical help for an imperfection in our brains that may manifest itself in any number of ways, including an emotional imbalance.

Since we are talking about emotions that cause the brain to make us less than what we could be, it's important we take a moment and discuss what the brain is physically, and how it works.

The more science learns about the human brain, the more obvious it becomes that there is a God, that He did create everything as He says He did in Genesis, and that He is a loving, planning, non-capricious God whose primary objective is order, stability, and building a way for his creation to know and love Him.

And since such a God exists, that is another argument against doing anything irretrievable because of your current feelings. Feelings change, your sense of self and value change, either through natural processes or through medication. So if you are feeling down right now, feeling as if life is not worth the effort, think back to when you did not feel that way and realize that through a little bit of work and, perhaps, a little bit of medicine, you can feel as well as you did before. This is not the time to do anything drastic.

## THE AMAZING BRAIN

Every thought you have, every emotion you experience, every movement you make, every bodily function you have originates in your brain. The rest of your body is only there to carry the brain around and keep it going. Without our brains we are nothing; it is the totality of what we are.

Of course, you have an invisible spirit that runs your brain, but still the brain has to be an extraordinary organ to do everything it's called upon to do. And it is extraordinary. It has the ability to store and access information—and some pretty complex information at that—pictures, maps, directions, rules, law. Some brains can literally take photographs of things and recall them perfectly later. The brain interprets 3-D images from two eyes, correlating all that information, then storing some of it for later use. It compares information with other information, images with other images. Have you ever wondered why a room seems familiar and later realize you've been there before? The image of that room had to have been stored somewhere. The brain has the ability to learn, to base actions on newly digested information and modify other information that has been found to be in error. It has the ability to make judgments and act wisely. And it can store information for a long time without losing a single bit of it.

On top of all that, the brain has the ability to feel and act emotionally. It has the ability to evaluate conflicting emotions—anger, fear, joy, sorrow, confusion—and determine which ones to act upon. And it builds complex and often hidden mechanisms to protect itself from emotional pain.

Of course, today is the age of computers—electronic brains. They do things that only people could do less than fifty years ago, and they do it extremely fast, switching speeds in the nanosecond (one-billionth of a second) range, and error free. But even today's smartest computer scientists and programmers are having trouble programming computers to do the things we easily do as a matter of course. There is a whole field of computer science dedicated to artificial intelligence and virtual reality. Programmers are trying to create a computer that can see as we see, think as we think—and so far, they have only been able to scratch the surface.

Each of us has about a hundred thousand genes. We are in those genes. Our hair, eye, and skin color. Our height and our weight (or at least our basic metabolic rates). Even some of our personality traits are locked inside those little organs.

The brain is made up of neurons—about one hundred billion of them, to be exact. Neurons are the information carriers of the brain. Each neuron consists of a cell body with branching structures, called dendrites, that extend from the cell body like the branches of a tree. In general, the dendrites receive impulses from neighboring neurons and transmit them to the cell body of the neuron in which they are embedded. Also projecting from the cell body is a single tube-like fiber called an axon—which also has tiny branches at its end. Most axons carry nerve impulses away from the cell body to the dendrites of other neurons. Axons may be only a fraction of an inch in length or they may be as long as several feet.

Glial cells surround the neurons, outnumbering them ten to one. These cells help regulate the biochemical environment within the brain, provide structural support for neurons, repair the central nervous system after injury, and supply chemicals and other substances essential for healthy functioning of the brain.

Your brain creates a process, such as writing your name, by connecting certain of these neurons through the tips of the axon and dendrites and firing tiny—we mean *tiny*—electrical impulses between them. Now, these axons and dendrites never actually touch. Rather the messages, or impulses, are transmitted by microscopic droplets of electrolytic "stuff." These particles of "stuff" are called neurotransmitters—specifically, serotonin, norepinephrine, dopamine, and the endorphins. The location where the "stuff" docks at the end of a dendrite is called a receptor. They are like space station rocket docks.

The space between where the axon of one neuron meets the dendrites of another neuron is called a synapse. Research confirms that synapses develop in response to the stimulus of learning and experience. A typical neuron has an average of about fifteen thousand intersynaptic connections. The impulse travels along a neuron chain at about two hundred miles per hour, and a neuron will process a message in about one-thousandth of a second. Both of these speeds are far below current computer speeds—but then a computer cannot have original thought.

## HOW YOUR BRAIN DEVELOPS

During the nine months of gestation, neurons are created at an average rate of 250,000 per minute. Yet as we age, after about fifty, we lose about 20 percent of our brain cells. But even for this loss, the brain remains vital, and experiences still mold its physical structure well into old age.

By age two, the number of synapses reaches adult levels and surpasses those levels between ages four and ten. A child's brain has twice as many neurons and twice as many connections between them and is twice as energetic as an adult brain. If you're a grandparent with young grandkids visiting, you know this is true—you've witnessed those synapses firing together all weekend long!

By about age sixteen, the brain assumes its adult form. As a person matures, the number of synapses falls dramatically as experience prunes the unused neural connections.

Now, there is no single, predetermined blueprint for the brain. More than half of all human genes, about fifty thousand, are somehow involved in laying the brain's foundation. And they all exert a powerful influence over learning ability and temperament. For instance, people who inherit a longer than usual version of a gene responsible for how the brain absorbs the neurotransmitter dopamine tend to be more exploratory, excitable, extravagant, and quick-tempered. And genes affecting behavioral traits are the most susceptible to environmental influences.

In a very real sense, our brains are computers that program themselves, which is another thing the silicon type cannot do. Our brains are an amazing creation of an amazing Creator!

## How the Brain Adapts

As a person's environment stimulates learning, the brain grows to meet the challenge. A college graduate will have up to 40 percent more neural connections (synapses) than a high school dropout. A child brought up in a learning-disadvantaged home can raise his or her IQ as much as thirty points by engaging in an intense, steady course of study. And raising the IQ cuts in half the risk for some forms of mental retardation and corrects common learning disabilities such as dyslexia.

As a person gains experience, the complex neuron network is continually revised in response to those experiences. Exercise, diet, and mental stimulation help keep the brain functioning at its peak.

Intelligence is not the only adaptation the brain can make. Texas health scientists discovered that when a stroke knocked out the part of the brain responsible for use of the fingers, adjacent regions of the brain gradually compensated. In response to physical therapy, neural circuits (synapses) devoted to the hand expanded into areas of the brain that had control of the elbow and shoulder.

The opposite is also true. If the brain is denied proper stimulation, the brain atrophies, and its neural connections wither like dying leaves. So—use it or lose it!

## AREAS OF THE BRAIN

The left side of the brain generally receives sensations and controls muscles on the right side of the body. It also controls speech and language in most people. The right side of the brain handles more visual and spatial tasks, such as drawing 3-D shapes.

Where human nature is concerned, the left side is believed to be more rational, logical, and mathematical, while the right side is more creative, emotional, and artistic.

Memory, concepts, and information are stored in the cerebral cortex. But memory and learning are partially handled by other parts of the brain known as the amygdala, hippocampus, thalamus, and the basal forebrain. Reactions to pressure and stress are in part the job of the brain system that includes the hypothalamus, cingulate gyrus, the pituitary gland, and the amygdala.

Moods and emotions are primarily controlled by the limbic brain, under the cerebral cortex. The limbic system includes the thalamus, hippocampus, amygdala, mammillary body, fornix, and the cingulate gyrus.

We're not trying to impress you with a lot of scientific terms. We simply want to point out that the brain is a complex, but organized system. If you were to see a system with a hundredth of the brain's capability sitting on the beach of a deserted island, would you think it evolved on its own?

We hardly think so. A design implies a designer!

But there is something else to consider about the brain. Something that eludes explanation.

Scientists are eager to attribute all brain functions to various chemical reactions between physical things—like cells and threads and chemicals. And since we are physical beings—flesh and blood and other elements—it seems logical to think that.

But there's so much more to us.

There are extraordinary acts of creativity and vision: Writers who create entire universes populated by strange and wonderful beings. Scientists who take something like bread mold and create penicillin. Psychiatrists who can look at behaviors and postulate the inner universe of the mind. A never-ending stream of creativity—great leaps of logic, even greater leaps of vision.

Where does the will come from? What drives us forward, even under tremendous pressures to shrink from the task at hand? What took a private from the landing craft on Omaha Beach at Normandy and drove him up that beach in spite of the bullets, the artillery, the mines, the death all around him? What part of the brain takes a woman in the late 1800s and drives her through all the obstacles and eventually brings her to becoming a physician? Incredible and powerful acts of will.

What part of the brain does God touch to fulfill His promise to "will and to do" within us (Phil. 2:13)? Where does our appreciation for beauty come from, or music, or mathematics, or the complex symmetry of art? None of these things can be explained in purely physical terms.

Something we can explain, though, are the times when things go wrong with the delicate balance in the brain.

## IMBALANCES THAT LEAD TO DEPRESSION

Some of the things that go wrong can be temporary imbalances; some of them can be long-term effects, which cause equally long-term imbalance. Some of the problems are in the genes, some are tendencies that are influenced by environment, others are imbalances produced regardless of environment.

### HYPOTHYROIDISM

Hypothyroidism occurs when the thyroid gland does not produce enough thyroid hormone, resulting in fatigue, body temperature problems, and depression. It has been generally known in the medical community for years that some cases of depression can be helped by thyroid medication. Researchers believe that depression can also affect the thyroid gland and sometimes contribute to the development of hypothyroidism. For some still unknown reasons, some bipolar I or II patients do not respond well to any of the top bipolar medications, but may respond well if thyroid medication is added.

### BIOGENIC AMINE IMBALANCE

As we have mentioned in our description of the brain, neuro-transmitters float in the synapse between two nerve cells. They are called the brain's amines, and the main ones are serotonin and norepinephrine. A decrease in these neurotransmitters is felt to be the major factor in depression. This belief is based on sound findings:

1. Drugs that have successfully treated depression are known to increase the level of brain amines.

2. A number of years ago a drug known as reserpine was used to treat hypertension (high blood pressure). Doctors observed that a number of people using this drug developed

depression. Further analysis showed that their brain amines were being depleted by the drug.

3. The breakdown product of the biogenic amines is catecholamine metabolites. The level of these chemicals is low in the urine of those suffering depression, implying low levels of brain amines in the brain.

4. Somatic symptoms (sleep, appetite, sex drive disturbances) occur when depression exists, and have been tied directly or indirectly to low levels of brain amines, which points to a strong biological component to depression.

The theory surrounding the physiological origins of depression is that those suffering from depression are either low in serotonin or norepinephrine, or both. This depletion can be caused by genetics, hypothyroidism, alcohol, marijuana, lack of sleep, or unresolved grief (especially bitterness or guilt). The depletion occurs most often due to emotional reactions to stress and stress-producing life situations (divorce, a tragic loss, internalized anger).

Bringing the brain amines back to appropriate levels can be accomplished by working through the tragedy, stress, or anger via counseling (Christian, we would hope), or by medication, or both. Which method is appropriate depends on the severity and the genetic issues involved.

Now that we have laid the foundation, in the next chapter we will take the next step in the process of dealing with genetically caused moods and mood swings—the medications and the discipline sufferers need to make sure the medications are working for them.

# 7

# MEDICATION
# FOR DEPRESSION

The vast majority of those who come to our clinics for treatment do not require medication. But of those who are diagnosed with major depression, a majority would benefit by taking antidepressant medication. Whether you require medication or not is between you and your counselor, but it is an issue you certainly want to discuss with him or her. Current medications, if properly prescribed, do a wonderful job in helping patients over the difficult times and returning them more quickly to normalcy. Of course, the medications only treat the symptoms of depression, not the root emotional causes. So the information and healing steps in this book and advice from a counseling professional are still essential in the healing process.

But what do all the possible medications do? In this chapter we will take a look at a wide variety of them, not because we expect them to be prescribed, but rather to give you a sound knowledge base so that you will better understand what prescription drugs are available and how they work.

## ANTIDEPRESSANTS AND OTHER MEDICATIONS

As we have been learning, depression can come from being trapped in one of the first four stages of grief: denial, anger turned outward or inward, or grief itself. In all cases this internalization brings with it a lot of internalized stress. For Warren, the stress of losing the love in his life; for Melinda, the threat of losing the love of her husband.

Internalized stress causes adrenaline to be released. This increase in adrenaline comes in two flavors, adrenaline (epinephrine) and noradrenaline (norepinephrine). When stress is not dealt with, certain biochemical changes take place, which eventually cause depletion of noradrenaline (norepinephrine). If the stress continues, as it will when we engage in denial or bury our anger or grief, depletion occurs and the norepinephrine level becomes extremely low. Serotonin also becomes depleted from our brains.

Norepinephrine, serotonin, and dopamine are three of the most vital neurotransmitters in the limbic system of the brain, which controls depression and euphoria. When norepinephrine and/or serotonin drops to a certain level, depression now becomes physical and biochemical, not simply emotional. At this point, an antidepressant can be given; within two or three weeks the medication will probably relieve a good number of the depression's symptoms. It accomplishes this by blocking the presynaptic neuron from taking up the norepinephrine or the serotonin or both, thus allowing the norepinephrine and/or serotonin levels at the receptor to rise. With this increase in norepinephrine and/or serotonin, the shroud of depression lifts.

Other antidepressants work in other ways. For instance, amitriptyline (Elavil) is a weak inhibitor of norepinephrine uptake, but a strong inhibitor of serotonin uptake. Differences like this account for why some antidepressants work for some patients and other drugs work for others.

The norepinephrine level is also important because it affects the hypothalamus, which, in turn, affects the autonomic nervous system, which ends up producing several physical symptoms during prolonged stress—rapid heartbeat, ulcers, nervous stomach, and the like. And since the hypothalamus is also influential to the immune system, those with prolonged stress suffer more from colds and upper respiratory infections, or even death from severe illnesses.

## TRICYCLIC ANTIDEPRESSANTS

There are several tricyclic antidepressants: amitriptyline (Elavil, Amitril); desipramine (Norpramin); doxepin (Sinequan, Adapin, Zonalon); imipramine (Tofranil, Norfranil, Presamine); nortriptyline (Pamelor, Aventyl); and protriptyline (Vivactil). Dosage varies, but a typical dose would be 150 milligrams of Tofranil daily. Given at bedtime, the sedative effect not only helps the patient rest, but it conveniently wears off by morning. Not all antidepressants are sedatives. Vivactil acts more like a stimulant, while Elavil is even more of a sedative than Tofranil. Tricyclics are still used frequently in poorer countries, but less so in America because newer, safer antidepressants are being invented all the time.

## A NEWER ROUND OF ANTIDEPRESSANTS

When scientists began looking at emotions as merely biochemical reactions over twenty years ago, the market for antidepressants ballooned. New ones are appearing all the time. The latest crop include Celexa, Serzone, Paxil, Zoloft, Prozac, Effexor-XR, Wellbutrin-SR, and Remeron, and overall all offer fewer side effects than their predecessors.

For difficult cases, sometimes the dosage is laced with a small dose of an antiseizure medication (like Neurontin or Depakote) or a powerful antianxiety, antipsychotic medication (like Seroquel, Risperdal, or Zyprexa). Augmenting the dose with Synthroid (a drug used to treat hypothyroidism) may also help. Sometimes a sedative antidepressant (like Remeron) is added at night to an alerting antidepressant (like Effexor-XR or Wellbutrin-SR), which are usually given in the morning.

Even though these new drugs are touted as having fewer side effects, the ones they do have can be bothersome at times, so a physician must oversee taking them. They all require prescriptions.

Depakote, an antiseizure medication, has also been found to have stabilizing effects as well and has been found effective in combating bipolar spectrum disorders. The same is true of Neurontin and Tegretol. The antidepressants and the anti-seizure medications can also be very helpful in the treatment of chronic pain syndromes or to prevent migraine headaches.

## MAO INHIBITORS

Monoamine oxidase inhibitors (MAOs) are not used as much today because of their troubling side effects, one being elevated blood pressure. Monoamine oxidase is responsible for breaking down norepinephrine. And if you don't break it down, it stays around. In the 1950s these drugs were used to fight tuberculosis and were found to produce euphoria in some, which, of course, made them useful as an antidepressant.

Those taking them not only have to avoid a host of foods (cheese, chocolate, red wines, beer, meat extracts, and yogurt), but also many other medications—various cold remedies, nasal decongestants, and Novocain used by dentists, to name a few. We rarely prescribe them because of too many side effect risks.

## AMPHETAMINES

Amphetamines seem also to affect the level of norepinephrine in the brain and have been used as an antidepressant especially in the elderly. However, after about two weeks of feeling reasonably good while taking them, the user may be visited by another depression, this one possibly caused by the amphetamines themselves. Furthermore, they may be addictive, so their use as an antidepressant may not be all that spectacular. We never prescribe them.

## TRANQUILIZERS

Although this group of drugs is generally not considered an antidepressants, there are a couple that have antidepressant qualities. Generally the group is used to decrease anxiety and to attack psychosis (losing touch with reality). As such, they can at times actually foster depressions or even make depressions worse. Those that run contrary to the pack and seem to have antidepressant properties are Mellaril and Navane. We seldom use these any more because the newer atypical antipsychotic agents (such as Seroquel, Risperdal, and Zyprexa) are much safer.

## WHAT AFFECTS DOSAGE

Most psychiatric drugs are fat soluble and concentrate in the lipid tissues, so women, whose body tissues contain higher percentages of fat, generally need higher dosages than men. Also, those who smoke require more medication.

As it turns out, fasting is also an issue. When fasting, the blood sugar level increases excessively when psychiatric medicine is taken, making them actually quite dangerous. Maintaining a proper intake of food, therefore, becomes essential. Do not fast while taking psychiatric medications.

Taking various drugs concurrently can also be an issue. Barbiturates, for example, lower the blood level of the tricyclic antidepressants. Therefore, when the two are taken together, the dosage of the antidepressant should be greater. The same is true for expectorants that contain ammonia chloride and medications that lower the pH level, such as large doses of vitamin C. This is also true for major tranquilizers. Amphetamines such as Ritalin decrease the speed at which tricyclics are eliminated from the body, thus increasing their effect. Even antacids can have an effect on antidepressant dosages. They make it more difficult for tricyclic antidepressants to be absorbed.

Interestingly enough, the elderly have a compensating issue: they have more difficulty absorbing the drugs, but they also do not seem to need as much. Those with heart disease need to be careful as well, since tricyclic antidepressants can cause cardiac problems.

## VITAMINS AND HORMONES

For many years people have been taking vitamin B6 and certain thyroid preparations like Cytomel to combat depression. However, it is only the exceptional individual who responds positively. Some cases of depression will respond to a concomitant use of antidepressants with thyroid extract.

The jury is still out on whether estrogen has an antidepressant effect. However, we know it does help with hot flashes and atrophic vaginitis. But the newer SSRI antidepressants, which build serotonin levels in the brain, usually help prevent PMS, hot flashes, and headaches.

### MEGAVITAMINS

Again, the jury is still out on massive doses of vitamins to combat depression, but a lot of research is being conducted. Most promising are the antioxidants such as vitamins B and E, because they affect unstable chemicals in the body known as free radicals. Antioxidants are showing some benefit for emotional and physical health. But you should follow a physician's advice, because some people may have health problems from taking too many vitamins.

## ALCOHOL, TOBACCO, AND MARIJUANA

Alcohol is a depressant, so it is hard to understand why millions of people use alcohol to self-medicate when they are already depressed. But they do, and when they do, they cause a lot of damage. Alcohol sends about twenty-five thousand people to their deaths on our nation's highways every year. And more than ten million alcoholics are now destroying families and costing businesses incredible amounts of money; twenty years ago the cost had already reached twenty-four billion dollars annually. Alcoholics kill themselves seven times more often than non-alcoholics. Although alcohol lowers serotonin levels, thus causing depression, 70 percent of people with bipolar disorders abuse alcohol or drugs in an unfortunate, inept attempt to self-medicate their moods rather than letting a psychiatrist do it correctly with medication.

We have heard a lot about the dangers of smoking. Cancer and heart disease are a high price to pay for the mild euphoria and tranquilizing effects of tobacco. If you are a Christian, of course, there are scriptural admonitions about maintaining and nurturing our bodies, which are the temple of the Holy Spirit, and smoking certainly runs contrary to that. The newer antidepressant, Wellbutrin-SR (same as Zyban), can help people quit smoking.

Unlike cigarettes, marijuana provides its user with an enjoyable euphoria. So some people use it like alcohol to self-medicate their depression. But also like alcohol, the cost of using marijuana is high. It can damage the brain, the lungs, and change the personality. And while it's doing all that, marijuana is eroding the memory, altering chromosomes, and dampening the person's motivation. It also depletes serotonin, thus causing depression and making suicide more likely.

Although there are many people who would like to call this merely theory, the scientific evidence is striking. Experiments with monkeys show that there are immediate changes in behavior and brain wave activity, and after long marijuana usage, the changes become permanent. Research reveals that if it is used twice per week, the memory starts to go, sleep is disturbed, moods begin to swing, and the person generally works at a lower level. If at least two marijuana cigarettes a day are smoked for two years, the person develops permanently abnormal brain waves and corresponding behavioral changes, such as chronic lethargy and loss of inhibitions.

And what's worse, the toxins within the smoke accumulate in the brain and permanently alter the fatty tissues. These alterations turn out to be quite subtle and may go unnoticed until the damage is significant. Although it may bring temporary relief from depression, over the long haul the lethargy, serotonin depletion, and loss of motivation bring on even deeper depression.

If you are self-medicating using alcohol, tobacco, and/or marijuana, we hope we have convinced you that such a course, while offering some momentary relief from depression, leads to places all of us, particularly Christians, should avoid. If you have not quit already, we strongly urge you to, and if you're having trouble quitting, we urge you to seek help.

## THE PURPOSE OF MEDICATION

We have taken the opportunity to introduce you to a number of medications used over the years to battle depression. And since new and more effective medications are being developed all the time, it would be unwise of us to be too specific. Between the writing of this book and its appearance in stores, new and improved medications will probably be approved.

Whatever the medication, its purposes should remain firm: to increase the sufferer's level of the brain amines, serotonin and norepinephrine, thus giving the depression sufferer the time and energy to attack the underlying causes of the malady. Prozac builds serotonin. Wellbutrin-SR builds norepinephrine. Effexor-XR builds both. Some individuals have primarily a serotonin depletion, others primarily a norepinephrine depletion. Some people need both. The psychiatrist still has to guess which antidepressant will work best for each patient. There are no accurate blood tests yet to tell us which one you need. So if the first antidepressant you take does not work, don't give up; the second one probably will.

The issue for most patients is not to know exactly what the medication of choice currently is, but to find a knowledgeable psychiatrist who knows the strengths and weaknesses of the various alternatives available. Or to find a psychological counselor you trust to refer you to a competent prescribing psychiatrist or physician. During your appointment, do not be bashful about asking questions, both about his or her experience and what they expect the medication to do. After all, the wrong medication can harm you, so make sure you feel comfortable with the person prescribing it. Also, antidepressant medications take from one to ten weeks to build up serotonin and/or norepinephrine levels, so be patient.

If you are suffering from a major depression and may also be bordering on psychosis (losing touch with reality), the wrong antidepressant might tip you over the edge, making you more psychotic.

So, at your appointment, work openly with the psychiatrist, answering all questions as thoroughly as you can. One series of questions is particularly important: Along with your depression, do you find yourself engaging in any compulsive acts such as perfectionism, ritualistic behaviors, excessive handwashing, counting ceiling tiles (for instance), or checking the locks on the house three and four times before going to bed, or any other behavior that might be considered obsessive or compulsive.

If the answer is yes, then the stronger these behaviors are, the higher the dosage should be of a seratonin-building medication.

At the writing of this book most people suffering from major depression will do just fine on twenty milligrams a day of Prozac or Paxil, or fifty to one hundred milligrams a day of Zoloft. But with depression and obsessive-compulsive behavior, higher doses of any of these three (or some other) medications may eliminate the depression along with the obsessions and compulsions. (Obsessive-compulsive disorder is usually genetic, but people with OCD can live normal lives on these meds if they take them lifelong.)

## TEMPORARY MEASURES

Medications for environmentally caused moods and mood swings are taken just for a short time, usually about one year (to prevent reoccurrence of the depression). Many antidepressants take several weeks to reach their maximum effect. The best way to inoculate yourself against recurrences of depression or irritability is to build a foundation of joy and connectedness upon which to construct the rest of your life.

So, the time has come to begin the journey to wellness. In Part 2, we will describe the step-by-step approach that will help you master your moods and bring a balance to your emotional life. Let's get started now.

# PART 2

# MASTERING
# YOUR
# MOODS

# 8

# PACKING YOUR BAGS FOR THE JOURNEY

If your moods and mood swings are reactions to emotionally charged life-issues, whether your reactions are causing minor depression, dysthymia, or major depression, the journey you will take to wellness, except for the intensity of it and perhaps its duration, is pretty much the same.

And if you are one of those with medical and genetic causes to your moods and mood swings, since you also experience normal moods—i.e., depressions and irritability—and perhaps even experience them more often because of your other moods, we suggest you begin your journey here as well. By developing methods to deal with these "normal" emotions, you will go a long way to decreasing your general level of stress. And since stress will aggravate your genetically caused moods—deepen depressions, cause highs to break more frequently into irritability, extend the episode's duration—you will be helping yourself tremendously as you go through the steps necessary to tackle them.

The first thing you need to do is something that sounds simple but provides an important shift in perception: admit you're in a mood.

## PREPARING FOR THE JOURNEY

Admitting that you are actually in a mood seems to go without saying. But it doesn't. It must be said. But more than said, it must be thoroughly believed. If you are depressed, say, "I'm depressed." If you're irritable, say it. Admit it. And when you do, internalize the meaning of what you're saying—that your negative emotions and reactions to those emotions are being caused by a removable emotional parasite.

Saying it means a lot.

It identifies what you're going through as abnormal. This depression is something that should not be. It's not who you really are. It's something that has come and taken up residence inside you, or is a shroud covering you, but it's not you—not in any way, shape, or form. It's an unwanted guest.

Now, saying this is doubly difficult for the dysthymic person. If you have been suffering from that malady, you have been depressed for a long time, possibly for most of your life, certainly for at least two years. Depression, in your mind's eye, *is* you. You are the Eeyore (Winnie the Pooh's chronically depressed friend) at parties and at work. People may have even commented on your constantly down demeanor—"Buck up, guy. Things just can't be that bad." Or "Nothing makes you smile does it?"

So you suddenly realize that the depression is not you, that the gray fog shrouding your emotional field is something that can be lifted. That notion may be hard for you to swallow, let alone own and use as a foundation for growth. If you are having trouble with the concept, then take your time with it. Say it to yourself a number of times. Begin to look at how your depression affects your life and capsulize your depression. Visualize it as a shroud, or a wet blanket, or even as a person working to manipulate your feelings and reactions. Soon you will believe that indeed your mood, your depression, is just that—an unwanted, thoroughly unwelcome visitor who has outstayed his welcome and needs to be thrown out by his coattails. Happiness can become a choice.

Getting to this point is not an academic exercise. It is important. For when you look at your mood in this way, you allow for the possibility of taking the next steps.

Not the least of which is to allow yourself to mistrust your feelings and where they might be taking you. Even though Brenda's moods were genetically caused, she found this admission very helpful. As we have already seen, mornings were always difficult for her when she was in a mood. Any little thing the kids did caused a flash of anger and a desire to lash out at them. But when she admitted to herself that she was in a mood— that that particular morning was under the shroud—those flashes of anger became instantly suspect, which made her desire to react suspect as well.

"I'm in a mood," she would say to herself. "Should I really be angry?" Her mistrust brought restraint. Perhaps after she looked at the situation she found that the anger was appropriate, but having stopped, she now had more control and her reaction was no longer to destructively lash out.

Or perhaps when you look at the situation, you find the anger is not appropriate and you temper the emotion, maybe reject it all together. The admission that you're actually in a mood is the first step to this kind of control.

There's more. Encapsulating the mood, making it a "thing," an unwelcome visitor, allows you to look at the unhealthy feelings as symptoms instead of reality. Depression in particular can take a deep toll on your sense of self. Every time Melinda made a simple mistake, for example, she became stupid in her own mind, an idiot, someone hardly fit to live. When she burned the toast, she became someone who couldn't do anything right. If she left out the snack pack of cookies in her eight-year-old's lunch box, she became an unfit mother who should turn herself into the authorities.

Warren, too, battled his sense of self bitterly. Instead of someone who came in second in a contest for a new job assignment, Warren became a loser, someone destined for the occupational junk heap. A mistake at work pushed him into valleys of inadequacy. "How could anyone worth anything do something like that. What kind of person am I?" It would not be so bad if these messages only ran once, or even twice, but they are always played on a never-ending cycle, chipping away at the sense of self-worth like a jackhammer.

But now when Melinda leaves the cookies out, she hears that message and says, "That's my depression talking. Not me." When Warren takes a call from a disgruntled customer and he can't seem to calm the person down, instead of launching into a diatribe of self-recrimination, he simply says, "Dysthymia's calling. I won't answer." Suddenly the messages lack validity. After all, they're coming from someone who doesn't like you, who wants you to fail, who wants to sap the strength from you—certainly not from a God who loves you. And He is really the only one you should be listening to anyway.

Encapsulating your moods also gives you the permission you need to unashamedly seek help. Your moods are just like a case of the flu, or your emotions' equivalent of a hangnail. When you have the flu, you have no problem buying a remedy or going to the doctor—there's no shame in trying to find a cure. Well, there's no shame in seeking help for your mood swings. Warren once told Dr. Meier, "I began to look at my dysthymia as a boarder, one I needed the sheriff's help to evict. And each bit of help it would ask for, I would look at as a sheriff's deputy sent to help me." Perhaps you are not into playing cops and robbers, but the principle is sound. If your moods are no longer a part of you but are there manipulating you, then there's no shame associated with them—and getting help to deal with them can be as easily justified as Warren calling the sheriff.

Viewing your moods in this way also allows you to see happiness as the reality—the choice. That was important to both Melinda and Warren. Melinda was so far down that she was beginning to think happiness was something she would never see again—that the listlessness and demoralization were now going to be her constant companions. But when she began to see her depression as that unwanted visitor, she could easily picture happiness returning when her visitor left. Happiness became her reality and her depression became something that was just clouding it.

For Warren, the shift became more difficult. He was not sure what happiness really was. Oh, at times he had felt pretty good—relatively—but even during those times there was always a sense of foreboding, a sense that things weren't quite right, that these moments of happiness were really stolen. He felt such moments would suddenly be reappropriated by their owner and he would be back where he belonged—in his mind, back to nowhere. So to tell himself that happiness was his true reality was a little tough.

What Warren finally did was to remember his happiest moment. He was eight and in Cub Scouts. The next-door neighbor was also in Cub Scouts, and his mother was one of the leaders. Seeing all the kids gather every Wednesday afternoon in the neighbor's backyard was too big a thing not to become a part of. And since it was right next door, he would not have to bother his mother to take him. So he joined. Begrudgingly, his mother shelled out for the uniform and the book and now and again some supplies; but she did not get much involved in scouting. Nor did his father, who was away a lot. So most of what Warren did there—the boy stuff and working toward the merit badges—he did for himself.

After being a scout for about six months, Warren earned a badge for forestry. He had to gather bark samples from at least ten local trees, place them on a board, and, along with a brief description of the particular tree, label them. This was not an easy project for an eight-year-old, and except for a little help from the neighbor lady, he did it on his own. After his project had been authenticated by somebody he had never seen before, Warren received his merit badge at a special award ceremony at the end of the Wednesday meeting. Just as he was being handed the little cloth badge, his father walked in. His father never smiled—it was just one of those things—and he didn't smile this time. But at least he had come. Warren found out later that the den mother had asked him to, and since he was in town—well, what the heck. But seeing him walk in at just that moment caused Warren's little heart to balloon with joy.

That moment became Warren's definition of happiness— that ballooning of the heart, that sense, albeit fleeting, that he really was loved. If you're having trouble redefining happiness for yourself, do what Warren did. Find a moment back there somewhere that was happiness, and in the magic of your imagination, expand it into a life that is waiting for you—a life that is your reality.

Defining that new reality also validates your struggle to achieve it. Your journey now has a valid and achievable destination. No longer is fighting the battle just an exercise. You have a goal and that goal is real—to become involved in the kind of relationships and life-style that will naturally bring happiness and fulfillment.

And when you validate the goal and the struggle, you gain a true sense of achievement with each step that brings you that much closer to your goal.

Finally, and very important, by simply telling yourself you're in a mood and that someday this mood will pass, you invalidate any desire you have to do anything permanent that has its roots in your mood. And that could mean any number of things. Suicide, certainly. But there are many other permanent life changes that can be made as a perceived way to make you feel better—marriage, divorce, having children, quitting your job, running away from home. If you are contemplating any of these things, the realization that you're in a temporary stop on a long journey should help you stave off thoughts of any permanent change. Now, that does not mean that as you work through the process you might not come to the conclusion that a permanent change is necessary. That's entirely different. A change that comes about through this kind of analysis truly is being made to make you feel better. It's a change that would affect the root cause of your moods and mood swings, the goal of which is to redirect your emotional and/or spiritual footsteps, rather than an attempt to mollify a symptom at the surface of the problem—which invariably leads to different, and perhaps even more severe, problems.

So after this first step of mood-admission, the next step is to clarify any reasons you might still have for inaction. You have to now ask yourself the question: "Is there anything about my moods and mood swings I like?"

## Hanging onto Your Moods

Emotions have many helpful purposes, and one of them is that they are part of your self-defense or survival mechanism. Moods are God-given signals for us to make constructive behavioral decisions. But not acting on these mood signals—allowing them to linger and infect us with prolonged unnecessary emotional pain—is a mistake most of us make from time to time. If you feel threatened, fear gets your feet moving; if attacked, anger mobilizes your defenses. These kinds of emotions have important jobs to do. The fact that you're depressed, or irritable, or experiencing some other protracted emotion might actually have some perceived benefit to you. By dealing with it, that benefit evaporates, and you might not be anxious for that to happen.

What follows are four common benefits various clients have derived from their moods and mood swings, and a discussion as to why those benefits sometimes become no benefit at all.

## AVOIDING RESPONSIBILITY

Melinda frequently relied on her moods as a "legitimate" way to avoid responsibility. Lying around and letting the rest of the world deal with itself appealed to her (we'll get to why later), but giving that ability up became a stumbling block. After all, with no responsibility came no criticism and no hassles. If people did something themselves, then when it was wrong, they had no one to blame but themselves.

The only way Melinda was able to push that block out of the way was to begin looking at her responsibilities as God-given. Making her kids' lunches was a responsibility God gave her when He gave her kids. The same with making the bed and cleaning the bathroom. God had given her these jobs. And not doing what God has given you to do can cause problems.

"As depressed as I was," Melinda told Dr. Meier, "I needed all the blessings from God I could get just to stay afloat. I began to realize that He probably felt a certain obligation to keep me, as His child, at a certain level of blessing—keep me breathing, keep my family together, my marriage intact—but greater blessings were probably being withheld. How could He bestow the fullness of His blessing when I was not doing what He had been blessing me for? So I began fulfilling my responsibilities. Begrudgingly at first, but then I began to receive the warmth from those I was doing them for, and some of my reluctance melted away."

Melinda still encountered reluctance and, as promised, we'll deal with that a little later in the process. But Jesus said His yoke was easy, His burden light. He never expects us to do too much—just a few things well.

Obtaining God's blessing was just one of the reasons Melinda found. Another, even more important, one was that her responsibilities involved those close to her. When she did not make lunch for the kids, the kids did not have good lunches. When she did not clean the house, her family lived in clutter. Those she loved suffered. By considering this, Melinda was actually making an important shift—she was beginning to look outward again.

Another common benefit came from Warren: when you're in a mood, people treat you with kid gloves.

## THE KID-GLOVE TREATMENT

When you are depressed, those closest to you neither want to add to your depression, nor do they want to cause you to become irritable. So they walk on eggshells around you. They choose their words carefully and try their best never to upset you. Being treated like royalty is not all that bad. But all their concern can quickly turn to contempt for you, and all the gentleness can be quickly replaced by neglect. In either case, your relationships can be severely damaged when such control tactics on your part cause resentment and a desire for revenge—people can hardly wait for you to get what you deserve. And one of those things you deserve is to be alone an awful lot.

Although Brenda did not get this next one too often, she voiced it as a benefit to her depressed moods: depression allows you to sit life out and remove yourself from the busy pace.

## DROPPING OUT

The Christian life is hectic. There is very little time to rest.

However, it is also rewarding as you see the fruits of your labors further God's kingdom. So when you're relieved from the fast pace, you're also relieved from the reward. One of those rewards may be more interesting work given to you by God.

Warren found this true at church. A guy put together a small men's accountability group—five guys who got together every other week to support one another and hold each other spiritually accountable—and was soon given the entire men's ministry to oversee. "That could have been me," Warren is quick to point out. "I'm every bit as smart as that guy is. But I wanted to withdraw, to become part of the woodwork. I saw that as an advantage. It wasn't. I could have benefited from the accountability group but still had the courage to turn down the extra jobs at church that I clearly don't have time for yet."

Another perceived benefit of moods and mood swings is unique to those with genetically caused bipolar spectrum disorders: they like the highs.

## ENJOYING THE HIGHS

Brenda, whose highs were on the low end of hypomanic, voiced this one as did Wendy, although Wendy was also quick to point out the negatives. Her highs were on the medium to high side of hypomanic. Brenda saw negatives, too, but they did not hurt all that much, certainly not enough to turn her against the overwhelming sense of excitement and well-being her hypomanic episodes brought with them—that sense of bursting with creativity and the ability—and desire—to take on the world.

"It's incredible," Brenda told Dr. Minirth. "I suppose it's what people on drugs feel. It can be quite addictive."

And along with that, quite disruptive. So the goal in treating the bipolar spectrum disorders, as we will see when we work through that process later in the book, is to bring the sufferer's life more into balance while still maintaining enough of the person's energy so that she, in a very real sense, has the best of both worlds.

Melinda was the one who voiced this last benefit: "When I'm depressed there's very little requirement to work on relationships."

## NEGLECTING RELATIONSHIPS

Being depressed is the best reason in the world not to have to talk to anyone, especially your spouse. The best reason in the world to leave work early. To put the kids to bed early, without a story. Or maybe even to leave the family for a weekend alone—"so I can collect my thoughts." Relationships require work. You have to take the time to understand what people say, to forgive them their trespasses, to do things for them, to love them. All that takes mental, physical, and spiritual energy. And sometimes it just plain hurts. When the depression ends, you will again be expected to make those relationships around you work. Not only will other people expect it, but God will expect it too. God expects it because He knows we can only experience joy in our lives when we are lovingly connected to Him and to quality people.

It can be effectively argued that relationships are one of the reasons God put us here on earth. To raise our kids in the fear and admonition of the Lord, to earn the right to share the gospel with our family and neighbors, to be a life-witness to others, to love and be loved. You can't love if there's not a relationship. So by stepping back from relationships, you're denying your most important purpose in God's kingdom. You don't want to do that, do you?

The last things we will do to prepare for our journey concerns another Person who will be taking the journey with us—that Person who has said He will never leave us or forsake us: God.

## INVITE GOD TO GO WITH YOU

As we discussed earlier, your moods and mood swings give you a warped picture of God. Instead of a loving Father intimately involved in your life, He is an ineffective, distant uncle. Now is the time to begin treating Him as what He is—Someone who loves you and has promised that if you love Him, all things will work to your good. So during this time of preparation, invite Him along. Go to your knees in prayer and ask Him to be right there with you every step of the way. Ask Him for strength and wisdom, for courage and help—let Him know that you can't make the trip without Him. From now on, He's not only a big part of your life, but the most important part. You really are helpless and hopeless without Him. It's the human condition.

And while you're doing that, let Him know that as far as you are concerned, you want what He wants, that "Thy will be done" will be the byword of all your work, that His timing will be your timing, that the lesson He wants you to learn will be the one you do learn. And as He walks with you, if He should point out anything in your life that needs correcting—things you're doing wrong, habits you need to break, relationships you need to eliminate or new relationships to foster—waste no time in doing it. After all, He's in charge of your journey to wellness because He, to a very large extent, *is* your wellness.

There are literally hundreds of Bible verses that will give you strength during this time of growth—some of them painful—and we'll point many of them out to you as the process unfolds. But for now, allow us to suggest just a few that may be of value during this time of preparation.

If you ever doubt that the Lord wants you to deal with your depression, your irritability, and your nagging sense of worthlessness so you can experience the fullness of joy, refer to Isaiah 55:12, "You will go out in joy and be led forth in peace; the mountains and hills will burst into song before you, and all the trees of the field will clap their hands" (NIV).

And Psalm 118:15, "Shouts of joy and victory resound in the tents of the righteous: 'The LORD's right hand has done mighty things!'" (NIV). Then John 16:22, "But I will see you again and you will rejoice, and no one will take away your joy" (NIV).

At times, the pain may be so great and the work so hard that you find it difficult to believe that God truly loves you. He does, and in the following verses (among many, many others) He tells His people so.

First, the most familiar and poignant: "For God so loved the world that he gave his one and only Son, that whoever believes in him shall not perish but have eternal life" (John 3:16 NIV). But what of it, right? What has He done for you lately? Is that the thought swirling around inside you? He has done a lot for you, and according to Deuteronomy 7:13, He plans to do a lot more. "He will love you and bless you and increase your numbers. He will bless the fruit of your womb, the crops of your land—your grain, new wine and oil—the calves of your herds and the lambs of your flocks in the land that he swore to your forefathers to give you" (NIV).

And as the pages turn and the work draws out and you wonder if it's all worth it, you begin to ask yourself: "What if I just stopped here? I'm okay right here. I don't have to get all the way there." Then take a moment to reflect on Proverbs 15:15, "All the days of the oppressed are wretched, but the cheerful heart has a continual feast" (NIV). That's where God wants you—He wants you to have that cheerful heart, and He wants you to believe what He tells us in 1 Timothy 6: "But godliness with contentment is great gain" (NIV).

So every time you get a little down, a little over worked, and a lot ready to quit—call upon God. Ask Him for strength to go on and take the next step, or the courage to slow down and delegate some of your work if you are overcommitted. A balanced life!

Which, of course, is what we're going to consider now. In the next chapter you will work on finding the root cause of your mood.

# 9

# FINDING THE ROOT CAUSE

Steve Arterburn's neighbor is an avid gardener. Since she lives in California, her garden blooms all year, and she is forever among her flowers digging, planting, feeding, and watering. Because of her efforts her garden is a wonder—brilliant with reds and blues, yellows and purples. Why is her garden so beautiful? The obvious answer is that she works hard at it. But that answer is only partially right. The rest of the answer is that she solves her garden's real problems. When the leaves begin to droop, she does not just cut them off, she waters the plant. When she finds aphids, she does not just brush them away, she sprays and gets completely rid of them. She goes after, forgive the pun, the root causes of her garden's problems. So the problems, rather than being masked or temporarily assuaged, are actually solved.

And that's what we are going to do in this chapter: help you identify the root causes of your moods and mood swings. We're going to find out what is really causing Melinda's depression. If we can pinpoint the source of Don's minor depression, perhaps we can minimize the chances that he will experience another. As we work with our sample case studies, we want you to work with us, taking the questions and the methods we apply to them and applying them to yourself.

## A LOOK AT THE FAMILY YOU CAME FROM

One thing our gardener has found is that no matter what you do to a plant, if you don't have the right soil and the right elements in the soil, the plant will not thrive. The same is true for people. Our soil, the family we were raised in, has a lot to do with how we face life in later years. So the first thing we will do is examine our family relationships. Psychiatry research indicates that for most of us, 85 percent of our adult attitudes, behaviors, and ways of looking at life were formed during our first six years of life.

On her second session with Dr. Meier, Melinda came alone. She again entered the office with that telltale sense of slowness, gripping Dr. Meier's hand listlessly, and sinking into the couch as if all her hopes and dreams, and all the emotions surrounding them, were sinking too.

"So," Dr. Meier began, sitting on the chair opposite her, "how's it going?"

"Not much has changed. I don't like life much."

"I see that in you."

"It shows then," she said, with a hint of sarcasm. "I was thinking people saw me as pretty bubbly, effervescent even."

"You're kidding, right?" Dr. Meier quipped.

"I'm kidding," she said. "So what do we do today?"

"We're going to go back to the wondrous days of yesteryear. Things that happened as far back as you can remember."

"Ah. Like analysis."

"Sort of. I believe that much of what we are now is because of what happened to us before we were six."

Melinda shook her head. "I haven't been depressed since I was six."

"No," Dr. Meier agreed. "But the groundwork was laid back then. What has caused you to react in this way today was probably put in place back then. If we can root that out—get it out here so we can take a look at it—we'll be able to move on. Make some decisions. Get you over this thing."

"Okay," Melinda said, with not much effort. "Why not?"

Dr. Meier got ready to take notes.

Now, as Dr. Meier asks his questions, think of them as aimed at you. Get a pencil and paper and answer them for yourself. Then, later, as he leads Melinda through the analysis of her answers, you'll be prepared to make the same analysis for yourself.

"Where were you born?" Dr. Meier asked.

"Gallup, New Mexico," she replied, with mock importance.

"Near the Navajos?" Dr. Meier said. "Drove through there once. Took my family to see the Grand Canyon in nearby Arizona."

Melinda only nodded. "My dad worked on the reservation—for their utility company. In personnel. Then did the same for the Navajo government when I was a little older."

"Was he Navajo?"

"He said he had a little in him. But I always thought he was lying about that. He said he liked that part of the country. He was a no-frills person and there aren't many frills out there. I think it was the only job he could get around there after college."

"What was your dad like?"

"I said it," Melinda said, sinking even further inside herself, if that were possible. "He was no-frills. Came home from work, read his magazines—he liked *Field and Stream* and the various hunting magazines—watched some pretty fuzzy television (this was before cable), and went to bed. Mom always said he was born out of time. He would have been a lot happier riding in that stagecoach with John Wayne."

"So he wasn't very happy. Is he still alive?"

113

"Died about five years ago. Lung cancer. He smoked like a chimney. Smoked even more after the dangers of smoking started coming out."

"What did you like best about him?"

"Like best?" That seemed like a tough question. Her eyes went up to the ceiling, then out the window. "His ability to escape from that place. Which is funny, because he could have left there anytime he wanted. But he didn't."

"I thought you said he liked that country."

"He said he did. But he never went out into the wild—out into that red desert he put us in. He read about hunting, but he never went. He read about fishing, but never did."

Dr. Meier cocked a brow. "He just sat there in front of the television all the time?"

"No. I'm sure not. But it seems like it."

Dr. Meier asked, "What did you like least about your father?"

"He didn't seem to care about us. I have a brother and a sister. Jim's the oldest. You'd think a guy that reads all the time about hunting and fishing would go hunting and fishing with his son. He didn't. My brother ended up going with some Navajo friends of his. He actually got pretty good at it. But dad never went."

"Did he ignore you?"

"Yes." Melinda nodded with some energy. "That about says it. I was into painting—actually learned how to sand paint from this Navajo guy I met at a restaurant. And I did some good things. Once I was shown at a small gallery in town, and Dad never even went to see what I'd done. He was like a zero in my life."

"When you said you admire his ability to escape into his magazines," Dr. Meier asked, "is that something you wanted to do? Escape?"

"Sure—a person can only take so much red rock."

How about you? Are you answering the questions? They're pretty straightforward. At this point you need to be answering questions about your early home life as it revolved around your father. Take a look at him as a human being with both good points and not-so-good points, and note how both affected your view of the world growing up. As you answer, try to do two things: (1) be as detailed as memory serves, and (2) be brutally honest. Glorifying someone is of no use to you now, nor is vilifying. If you don't want anyone to read what you're writing, just hide it or burn it later.

Dr. Meier took a moment to jot a note. "What about your mother? How do you remember her?"

"She's still alive," Melinda said, her energy level still pretty low. "When Dad died, she left Gallup and went to Flagstaff, Arizona. Pretty place. Lots of snow in the winter. Too much snow to visit her in the winter. My blood got too thin in Gallup. I don't know how she takes it."

"Do you visit in the summer?" Dr. Meier asked.

"Not often. I was hoping she'd move our way, or at least to California, where Jim and my sister are. But she didn't."

"Were you two close?"

"You know—I guess. Mom was mom. She was always there for us, but I can never remember her smile. We never wanted for anything, but I can never remember her having fun with us. She never failed to support us in anything we did—she came to my gallery showing, for instance—but I don't remember her encouraging or guiding us. We were always told to do our homework, but she never talked to us about what we ought to be doing when we grew up. I guess when it's all boiled down, Mom always did her chores very well. And we were one of her chores."

"Was God in the home?"

"Through Mom. We always went to church and Sunday school. But again, it was the right thing to do, so we all did it. I never remember her dealing with God in any way. I'm sure she believed He was there, but He was never on her to-do list. I always saw God as off in the distance, not really caring about me that much."

"Sort of like your mom and dad were, right?" Paul asked.

"I learned from experience and from my studies of psychiatry research that when you were three years old and saying your goodnight prayers, you were thinking, 'Dear Heavenly version of my earthly father (and mother)."

"That's why you have trouble, Melinda, seeing God as He really is—trouble connecting to Him. You have a warped view of Him—thinking He is like your parents. We all do that to some extent. You'll very rarely meet someone who calls himself an atheist who had a great relationship with both parents growing up. As a psychiatrist, I almost never see it. Melinda, was there any arguing in your home?"

"No. Things might have been more interesting if there had been. Everyone sort of did what they were supposed to."

"No one got in any trouble growing up?"

"No. Everything just moved along—we put one foot in front of another. Everyone did his duty."

"So you looked to your mother for provision, but not for love. Where did love come from?"

Melinda shifted her weight a little uncomfortably. "I guess it came from Don."

"Did you two grow up together?" Dr. Meier asked.

"No. In fact, we didn't know each other very long before we ran off together. I was working as a waitress at that family restaurant, the one with the sand-painting guy, and Don came in. He had gotten a short-term job on the reservation working on some roads or something. He had just graduated from high school and was doing a little traveling. We fell in love and that was that. We headed for the big city—Albuquerque—and decided to go to college. We actually stayed together all the way through college—never broke up once—and then graduated. After marriage came kids and his career, and that pretty much brings us to the present."

"How often do you talk to God?" Dr. Meier asked. "And how often do you feel like He's saying something to you?"

"God?" She mulled it over for a moment. "I believe in God—in Jesus. I think we talked about that last session. What do I think of God? That's a dangerous question."

"Is He active in your life? Or is He disengaged from your life?"

"I'd say He sort of winds things up," she said, her eyes on Dr. Meier, "then lets them go. I don't think He's as active in people's lives as people like to think He is. I think it's pretty well up to us to make life what we want it to be. I guess you're right about us seeing God through 'sunglasses' the same shade as our parents."

"So God is out there somewhere watching," Dr. Meier asked. "If you get into trouble, you're pretty much on your own. Responsible for getting out of it the best way you can."

"Yeah, I guess." Melinda hadn't moved much at all as she answered the questions. Even now her eyes were lifeless.

You can easily see the ground this has covered: father, mother, and God—what you feel about each, how you see each of them now, and what impact each has on your life both then and now. We are all born with a father-vacuum, a mother-vacuum, and a God-vacuum, and those early relationships profoundly impact our lives. But we can always find ways to heal those early wounds. We can always form new quality relationships, but we also must grieve all of our past and current losses. So let's take a good look now at how we can help ourselves get through some very necessary grief processes.

## THE FIVE STAGES OF GRIEF

You may have heard about these stages when considering how you might react to the death of a loved one or some other great loss. Certainly, working your way through the five stages of grief is imperative in that situation, but it's also imperative in other situations as well.

Whenever anything negative happens to you, be it your pen running out of ink, a flat tire, or, indeed, the tragic loss of a loved one, in order to deal with the situation in a healthy manner, you have to work your way through the five stages of grief. Of course, for a pen running out of ink, the journey through the various stages is quick, but that does not change the fact that each stage must be worked through.

Let us quickly outline the five stages.

### DENIAL
"Oh, this can't be happening. Surely this isn't happening. There has to be another explanation. Pens don't just run out of ink."

### ANGER OUTWARD
"You did this to me. You're the one who gave me this pen and here it is out of ink. Have you no brains? Don't you check your pens before you go out of the house with them?"

### ANGER INWARD (GUILT, SHAME)
"No, it's my fault. I should have carried two pens. I knew how important signing this document was. How stupid. How much does a BIC cost, for crying out loud? I'm a cheap, cheap idiot."

## GENUINE GRIEF

"Oh, well, I just have to accept this. It's out of ink, and before we could get another pen they changed their minds. What a shame. Just leave me alone for a moment and I'll work through this."

## RESOLUTION

"Okay. It's over. It was difficult. But I still have my health, and life is truly good. I'm sure I'll be just fine."

We realize that explanation was a little tongue-in-cheek and, of course, there's nothing tongue-in-cheek about grief. For not only is grief the response to something negative occurring in life, something none of us want, but depression—all three types we've talked about, major, minor, and dysthymia—can be (and usually is) caused by the individual not working completely through the five stages of grief. In a very real sense, the individual has gotten "stuck" in either steps one, two, or three, and languishes there in depression. If we know and understand these stages, we can actually speed up and complete these processes and become "good grievers," thus spending much less time grieving when we do suffer inevitable losses. And we can totally avoid clinical depressions, since they are usually the result of getting stuck in one of the first three stages of grief.

In the next chapter we are going to take each of our study cases through those five stages and identify what steps they have made to get "home" to happiness.

# 10

## GETTING STUCK IN ONE OF THE STAGES

Warren sipped a lukewarm, half-flat Coke as he walked around the brightly lit, hastily erected rides at the small county fair. He walked alone, but that did not mean there were not other people around. Although the carnival was not as crowded as it would be later, after people came home from work, a number of kids and a few adults still wandered about. For some it might be difficult to come to a place like that alone. It seemed like a place best appreciated by groups—the more boisterous, the better. But Warren preferred it alone, like he preferred everything else. When he was in groups, the other people just wanted him to cheer up. "Have some fun, guy. Life's too short." He was not in the mood for that too often.

Curiously enough, Dr. Meier was on his way home from a speaking engagement and saw the cheerful lights on the swinging and swirling rides, and decided to stop and get some popcorn, and walk around for a moment, just to renew himself before getting home.

"Dr. Meier!" He heard his name being called. Turning, he found Warren waving his way.

"Warren. Good to see you." They shook hands and Dr. Meier led him idly toward a popcorn booth. "You come for the rides?"

"I just walk around. I've always been partial to these little carnivals. Whenever one comes to town, I spend some time in them."

Paul took a handful of popcorn and offered Warren some. Warren took a few kernels and popped them in his mouth. "What is it you like about these places?" Dr. Meier asked.

"Don't know," Warren said, the two of them drifting toward the games and the barkers calling at people to play them. "But I always end up walking around." A bell rang—someone had slammed a sledge hammer and sent the puck flying up. Warren flinched, his eyes finding the bell. "My grandpa loved to hit those things. He was a big man. Of course, I was only about five so I guess all men looked big. He sure liked to ring the bell. Always."

"How long have you been coming in to see me now?"

"A couple of months—I think."

"Twice a week. And you've never spoken of your grandfather to me before."

Suffering from dysthymia, Warren began coming to Dr. Meier after his pastor had used one of Dr. Meier's books, *Happiness is a Choice for Teens,* in his ministry and thought Warren could benefit from Dr. Meier's counsel. Over the past couple of months he and the doctor had been searching through his memory for some of the keys to his past, a past he did not embrace nor remember much about. But a past that was probably tangled tightly up with his present.

"Funny, huh," Warren said slightly puzzled. "I was just a kid when people said he died. Maybe he's like the studs in a house. They hold the place up but you never see 'em."

"That's quite profound. Mind if I use it sometime?"

"Go ahead," he said. "Coming here makes me think of him. Since my mom and dad split when I was so young, and neither one of them wanted me, I was shipped around a bit. My

Grandpa—Grandpa Dozi I called him. His name was Dozioski, but I was only four or five. He was great to me. He played with me and goofed around—and always took me to these carnivals when they came to town—a couple of times a year. Then he would take me to the county fair. I guess I hope to find him again one day."

"You said people told you he passed away," Dr. Meier said. "Seems a strange way to put it."

"That's the way it was. One day I was playing with him and the next day somebody I didn't know was telling me he died."

"Did you go to a funeral?" Dr. Meier asked.

"No. He was just gone."

"Like your mom and dad," Dr. Meier said, popping another handful of kernels into his mouth.

"I remember crying a lot and feeling like I was being kept from him. Like I'd been kept from everybody else I cared about." Warren looked up. "Pretty maudlin—but I guess that's what I am. Eeyores don't get what they want."

Dr. Meier nodded, "I think we might be on to something here, Warren. Why don't you come in the office tomorrow about eleven and we'll explore this a little more fully. In the meantime, enjoy the carnival and your grandpa's memory." Needing to get home, Dr. Meier left Warren there.

## WARREN'S DYSTHYMIA
### STUCK IN THE FIRST STAGE OF GRIEF: DENIAL

This is what Dr. Meier gleaned from their next few visits together.

When Warren was five or six, the one man in all the world that seemed to love him died. Since Warren was so young, he was not allowed to come to the funeral, and since no one wanted to hurt the child further, no one brought up his grandpa again.

Since little Warren had been deserted by his other two parents, his heart assumed that Grandpa had done the same. In his heart, his grandfather couldn't really be dead. How could anyone be so cruel as to take his grandpa away. "He just can't be dead," his heart kept saying. But in saying that, he was also saying that one more important person in his life had deserted him. From that moment on, Warren was locked in the first stage of grief—denial.

To stop denying, to accept his grandfather's death as fact, would be cutting off all hope of ever experiencing love again, he believed. A tragic admission. But just as tragic was the admission that came when his heart was unwilling to face facts. It was telling him that since he had been abandoned by his parents and his grandfather, he was not worthy of being loved. No wonder he trapped himself in denial—there was no way out. And by trapping himself there he pushed himself into a chronic depression. Facts were facts, he was just not worthy of happiness. Getting close to people now would "logically" result in more rejection and more pain, so the pain of loneliness, emptiness and "nobodiness" was the lesser of two evils in Warren's warped economy of love.

Dr. Meier enabled Warren to write a good-bye letter to his dead grandfather and place it on his tomb, weeping as he did so, thus breaking through his denial. He also reassured Warren that, even though some future attempts at intimacy may result in rejection, there are some good people out there who would love Warren unconditionally, just the way he was, for the rest of his life (and for eternity thereafter).

After Warren saw the validity of Dr. Meier's suggestion, the next step was to work his way through the remaining stages— the next steps of the process.

Does any of this ring true for you? If you are suffering from dysthymia, is there anything in your past that may have trapped you in denial—denial that a tragedy really happened, or that someone dear to you caused you great harm, or didn't behave or feel toward you as you would have expected? Denial is usually caused by being locked between two or more terrible choices—choices that hurt your own sense of self, or bring a sense of danger to your world of emotional safety. So, rather than admitting and taking yourself through the hurt, you step back from it and continually shake your head in disbelief.

If you've found that you have anniversary illness, where a particular time of year comes around and pushes you into a minor depression, look into your past and asked yourself, "What terrible thing happened to me during that time?" Perhaps a dear loved one passed away, or your parents split up, or a parent left, or some other tragedy befell you. And now, when that time approaches you slip into denial—you shut it out, unable to come to grips with it. This is very common but usually goes unrecognized because of denial.

If any of this is true, you need to work your way through denial and continue working through the remaining stages of grief to resolution and freedom from your depression. In the next chapter we'll walk you through those steps. If, however, this does not ring true for you, or perhaps you're not sure, then let's visit Melinda and see if her experience mirrors yours.

## MELINDA'S MAJOR DEPRESSION
## STUCK IN THE SECOND STAGE OF GRIEF: ANGER OUTWARD

Melinda sat in Dr. Meier's office on a warm Texas morning, her eyes distant, even more so than the last time she had come. She wore navy blue sweats, ones that probably had hung loosely on her at one time, but now clung more tightly. Her auburn hair was pulled back through a blue scrunchie into a ponytail and appeared to have been combed haphazardly.

"How are you feeling this morning?" Dr. Meier asked.

"How do I look?"

"Like you don't care?" Paul said.

"That's how I feel. I nearly didn't come."

"But you did," Dr. Meier pointed out. "Why?"

"Don will throw me out if I don't," she said. Paul had the distinct feeling that she believed her husband actually would do something like that. "I have to at least look like I'm trying to get better."

Taking her lead, Paul asked, "Tell me a little about you and Don."

Her expression actually changed—from one of sad indifference to just sadness. It was mostly in her eyes—a rise in the moisture level. "What do you want to know?"

"What was your relationship like before the depression started?"

"Wonderful," she said, without hesitation. But it wasn't a joyous word—there was a sense of loss to it, as if it were being placed in the past tense.

"What made it wonderful?"

Again without hesitation: "We trusted one another. I could tell him anything and he could tell me anything. We did things for one another. I would make his favorite dinners and he would plan romantic weekends. It was another world. So far from being in Gallup, New Mexico, you wouldn't believe it. We had truly escaped."

"So why are you willing to give all that up?"

Now her eyes became even more liquid, and the strain behind them revealed itself in streaks of crimson. "I don't have a choice," she said.

"You're talking about your depression? You say you don't have a choice about your depression?"

Her head shook. "No. He took it away from me."

Paul sensed the tears being dammed up behind those eyes. Although he still was not sure what she meant exactly, he did know that his question had pierced the depression's surface. The pupils of her eyes dilated. Her neck got red blotches. She no longer looked Paul in the eye, so Paul knew they were close to her root problem: repressed anger toward her husband, Don. "Tell me what you mean."

"Don. Don took it away."

"I have this feeling you want to tell me something, but you're holding back. Either you're afraid, or voicing it is too painful. I want you to take a deep breath and just say it. Get it out. Pretend it's a Band-Aid on a hairy arm and just give it a yank."

"Hairy arm. Right." The red blotches on her neck got redder. Her body's reactions were telling Dr. Meier much more than her words were. Her rage toward Don was buried deep within, possibly along with some unconscious anger toward God for not "fixing" Don. She took the deep breath. Maybe a longer, deeper one than she needed, but taking it gave her time to gather her thoughts—thoughts that Paul could see needed a lot of gathering. The words finally came out in a rush. "We had built up such trust. Our feelings were always safe with one another. We would never say anything that would hurt the other. Never."

"What did he say?"

"Nothing. That's the point. It was like my feelings ceased to exist. The compliments stopped. What can I do to make it better? What can I say? I feel like everything's slipping away and I have no ability to stop it. God has just abandoned me here. It's like I'm watching my children going down on a sinking boat and I don't know how to swim. And Don's the one who put them there. All I can do is watch. He just seems to have stopped loving me or showing me any attention."

"That's a frightening analogy," Dr. Meier said.

"And all of this has to be my fault. Don is usually such a good guy. It just has to be my fault. Has to be."

We realize this is an awkward place to stop, but there are a number of things to say here.

God tells us to get rid of our anger, not to let the sun set on it. Even if we are in the middle of giving gifts to the Lord and realize that we have a problem with our brother, we are to go and reconcile with our brother before proceeding. But Melinda didn't do that. Instead, she buried the anger. And what's more, the anger she buried that was initially aimed at Don then became redirected toward God ("God has just abandoned me.") and finally toward herself. She now became trapped in the third stage of grief—anger turned inward.

## MELINDA'S MAJOR DEPRESSION
### STUCK IN THE THIRD STAGE OF GRIEF: ANGER INWARD

Melinda is a perfect example of this inward-directed anger, and her earlier life set her up for it. Growing up in Gallup, she learned that there was no validity to her anger. Ignored by her father, no more than a chore to her mother, any display of emotion was of no consequence. When perhaps for the first time in her marriage the same thing was consistently happening to her again, she reacted as she had learned to react. She swallowed her anger toward Don.

But worse yet, she had assumed something else as she was growing up—that having her emotions ignored was her own fault. When we're little, the whole world revolves around us. We cannot even imagine a world without us in it. When things go right, it's because we demanded them to, and when things go wrong, it's our fault. We react as adults the way we learned to before age six (unless we decide to reprogram our brains with new and better "redecisions.") Since those same feelings were bubbling to the surface again, she thought they must have had the same cause—herself. Maybe Don was under a lot of pressure at work, maybe his reaction to her was because of something she had done, and maybe she wasn't so much angry as emotionally battered by her loss—the person she had escaped Gallup with, given her whole life to, was now abandoning her emotionally, just as everyone else in her life had abandoned her emotionally. And, anyway, she couldn't really put her finger on anything *he* had done. There had not been a big blow-up or a knock-down drag-out fight. Only little comments or brief times when he had ignored her; she could have misunderstood them all. So, unable to clearly define her anger or support it, unable to pin it on him, she simply buried the anger at herself and allowed it to go unexpressed and unsatisfied. She became stuck in the third stage of grief—anger turned inward—resulting in guilt and shame. Shame is usually false guilt—when you feel guilty, even though you haven't really done anything morally wrong. Melinda had been shamed with false guilt all her life.

Depression caused by anger turned inward is common. Many depressions are the result of repressed anger toward others, God, or self. As strong, independent human beings, a part of us is keenly aware that those close to us often cause us the most grief and deserve our anger. Yet another, sometimes stronger, part of us just cannot imagine that we are *not* at fault for every bad thing that's ever happened to us. Caught in the middle of these opposing emotional armies, we feel the anger but don't express it, then go on to believe we're at fault anyway.

As these forces war within us, we end up burying the anger—or fear, or confusion—and fall into a deep depression. And when these armies come together at the same time every year to commemorate a specific terrible event in our lives, anniversary illness is the result. Others stay depressed all year round, but dip ever deeper on the annual date of their worst hurt.

Does this sound like what's happening to you? As you deal with your depressed situation, do you find yourself saying or thinking, "This is all my fault"? Or, "If I'd only done (fill in the blank), I wouldn't be in this mess"? Or perhaps, "I always do this. I'm such a dope. I don't deserve to live"? If your parents ignore you or push you away as a child, they are giving you non-verbal "don't exist" messages. Your death wishes now may actually be in obedience of their nonverbal messages to you as a child. Do you choose to keep obeying these false messages, or will you choose the truth—that you deserve to live and enjoy life? If the tapes are spinning in your head, telling you how incompetent you are and how much better off you and the world would be if you were just a little smarter, a little more on top of things, a little more aware, a little more sensitive to what's going on around you, then your depression is probably the result of being trapped in the third stage. If that's true for you, the next step you will take is to free yourself and go on through the fourth stage to the fifth, resolution. In the next chapter we'll help you get there.

But if this doesn't ring true, if the tapes are saying something else entirely, then perhaps you're trapped with Don.

## DON'S MINOR DEPRESSION
### STUCK IN THE SECOND STAGE OF GRIEF: ANGER OUTWARD

Don sat in Dr. Meier's office. He wore a light summer suit and expensive, brown wing tips. Anxious, he perched uncomfortably on the edge of the couch and waited for Dr. Meier to speak first.

After the social amenities, Dr. Meier said, "You ended our last visit saying that you wanted to think about some things. Have you?"

"I didn't like our talk about my past. My mother was a saint. I didn't like the implications that she wasn't. You accused me of putting her on a pedestal."

"I made no implications. I just asked you questions."

Don looked at his shoes. "I know. But Mom was a saint. She worked her hands to the bone for us. I left my three younger brothers and sisters at seventeen so that I would no longer be a burden to her. That's when I met Melinda—when I was out trying to earn money to help Mom take care of our family. I didn't like you suggesting that there was something wrong there."

"Well, what brings you back then?"

"I did that thinking."

Dr. Meier nodded expectantly.

"I was mad at her."

"Your mother?"

"No. Melinda. I could never be mad at Mom. That's why I treated Melinda the way I did. I was mad at her."

Dr. Meier cocked a brow. "Why? What did she do to you?"

"Nothing. She did nothing. That was the point. She did nothing."

"Explain."

"It was about work—back then. A couple of months ago. Work suddenly got very difficult. It still is."

"In what way?" Dr. Meier asked.

"I handle some key accounts in the southwest, some of the big high tech companies. About the first of the year we had some competition that came on strong and I lost two very large accounts. Management told me if I lost another I'd be on the street."

"What kept you from talking to Melinda about that?"

"I didn't want to worry her."

"What did you think she might do?" Dr. Meier asked.

"Come unglued—make me feel like I couldn't do the job."

"Like you were suddenly a burden? Like you'd failed her? Like you said you felt around your mother when you were seventeen?"

"Yeah. I guess." Don began to appear more hostile, as if he had seen the implications of Dr. Meier's questions. "You think that's the way my mom would make me feel, don't you?"

We all transfer emotions from our parents to our mates to some extent, Dr. Meier explained. "Now, go on about being angry at Melinda."

Don nodded stiffly. "I was under such pressure at work. Working so hard to make a buck and keep the bills paid and the family going. And she was at home with the kids. The only pressure she had was to make sure she took something out of the freezer for dinner. It just didn't seem fair. I know it was wrong, but suddenly I just couldn't compliment her, could hardly look at her. Then she started going downhill, getting depressed, and I started getting madder at her—and trying to cover it up."

"You were jealous because you had it harder than she seemed to."

"Right. Families are supposed to work together—share the load."

"Your father deserted you as a baby," Dr. Meier said, reading a note he'd made to himself.

"Never did anything for us."

"Do you have any anger toward him?" Dr. Meier asked.

"How can I be angry with him? I never knew him. Mom picked him. Not me."

"So you have no repressed anger toward your mom or your dad, right? Only toward Melinda, who is safe and loves you pretty much unconditionally, right?" Dr. Meier pressed on. "How young was your youngest sibling when you left home?"

"Uh? Six," Don said. "Danny was six."

Dr. Meier nodded and made a quick note.

There are many reasons we might not be able to resolve anger. One reason can be that we're angry at someone we believe we should not get angry at—a person who has died, for example, or God, or a mother who has sacrificed her whole life for us. We find such anger repugnant. "What kind of person am I that I'm angry at God?" Or, in Don's case, "My mother's a saint who worked her hands to the bone for me, but made it so I had to leave my brothers and sisters when I was still a kid and go out and earn money for her. Why couldn't she have picked a better man, a better provider? Why did it have to all fall on me?"

That kind of anger we might deny. And when we find ourselves in a similar emotional situation, we do the same thing: we get depressed. Often it causes only minor depression because over the years we learn to deal with some of our anger, but it's a depression nonetheless. Don's depression was triggered by being stuck in the second stage of grief—anger outward—an unresolved anger at his mother (and his father), which he transferred unconsciously to his innocent wife, which triggered her own childhood dynamics in a painful chain reaction.

Does this ring true for you? Within the context of your depression, do you find yourself defending people you are supposed to love for doing things that might have caused you pain? Do you find yourself calling that person a saint, or the greatest person who ever lived, or some similar expression that goes far beyond what he or she really was? No one is perfect, and although all of us who know God are called saints, no one is a saint the way Don used the word.

But there is another face on this particular coin. If you are going around within your depression saying things like, "If he'd only done something differently," or, "If she'd only been more sensitive," you may be blaming someone for something, but unwilling or emotionally unable to do anything about it, and that outwardly directed anger is dragging you further and further down. Then, like Don, you are trapped in the second stage of grief, and getting trapped in either of the anger stages causes serotonin to be depleted from the brain, which causes depression.

If you believe you are trapped here, the next step is to work your way through this and the following stages and get to resolution. In the next chapter we'll help you do that.

## GETTING TO THE FOURTH STAGE: GENUINE GRIEF

Have you suffered a tragic loss sometime in the past—the loss of a loved one, the loss of a hope? In the society we live in, we are often told to be stoic about these losses. Perhaps we're told not even to cry at funerals, certainly we're told not to cry at the loss of a dream. That admonition to remain strong and without tears goes double for a man. Yet Jesus wept at the death of his dear friend Lazarus, and Joseph wept at the death of his father. Grieving at a loss is essential. Often, tears are essential. Grieving is what emotionally strong people do. Stuffing our grief is an act of the cowardly, of the emotionally weak, and of good people who were simply given horrible advice based on devastating cultural and family traditions.

Have you wept for that loss? If you haven't, those tears are still welling up inside you, and keeping them down may be the cause of your low-serotonin depression. Have you been holding those tears back, afraid to offend the living, or afraid just to be what you really are—a hurting human being who will deeply miss the person who has gone on before you? If that is true for you, have your cry, feel your loss, give the one who has passed on the tearful proof that he or she will be missed.

For those who have found themselves trapped in their grief at this stage, after they have allowed their emotions free rein, after they have had their cry—their deep, troubled, pain-purging cry—psychological tests have shown a marked reduction in depression. Grief is good, so practice "good grief" and flow with it every time a wave of sadness wells up within your soul for the rest of your life. Paradoxically, releasing those waves of tears will bring your life greater periods of joy in between.

We have brought you through the journey to find the root cause of your environmentally caused moods—your anger/shame-induced depression. If you still need to do a little work, take a moment to go through the following steps. And get connected to God and good people. You simply cannot make it through life alone.

- Analyze your life history. Determine those elements of your life that may have triggered fear, or anger, or feelings of abandonment, or any other emotions you would not associate with a loving family home life. Be honest with yourself and your memories. Remember: no one is perfect, and no one is entirely evil. Be as objective as you can with those in your past.

- Find the parallel between the life history you have assembled and your current situation.

- Determine which of the stages of grief you are dealing with.

- *Denial.* You cannot admit the tragedy happened, that it's real and it's everything your fears say it is. You can't believe someone you trusted was so evil, that he or she could betray you to that extent or fail to protect you.

- *Anger Outward.* You are angry with someone you believe you should not be. Or you're angry with someone and, for whatever reason, you are unable to resolve the anger.

That jerk in your past may not deserve your forgiveness, but turn vengeance over to God—He will repay the jerk. The jerk is not worth depleting your own serotonin for years, so release him emotionally to God.

- *Anger Inward.* If you feel guilt or shame and are continually blaming yourself for what you're going through, you have turned your anger inward. This can be true guilt for real but unconfessed failures, or false guilt and shame from past abuse.

- *Real Grief.* For whatever reason, you have not allowed yourself to work through the devastation of what has happened to you through tears and a genuine feeling of remorse. Remember to practice good grief and weep when you feel sad, so true joy and relief can follow. Don't allow yourself to get emotionally constipated and then fool yourself into believing the popular lie that if you are "strong" you will:

  a. suck it up

  b. pull yourself together

  c. pull yourself up by your own bootstraps

  d. tough it out

  e. hold back your tears

  f. just get on with it

  g. be a man (or strong woman)

  h. be spiritual by not grieving (even though Jesus told us to weep with those who weep).

The above are all acts of cowardice or ignorance, not strength!

Now that you have identified the root cause of your depression and begun to walk through the stages of grief, let's move forward to other steps that will help you on your journey to wellness.

# 11 MOVING PAST THE GRIEF

In the last chapter, you discovered whether you were trapped in one of the stages of grief. In this chapter, we will take you through that particular stage and on to the fifth stage, resolution. Remember that life is difficult, so all of us go through grief reactions many times in our lives. But clinical depression is totally avoidable if we do not get stuck in the grief process and if we take proper medications for genetic mood swings (or for severe environmentally caused depressions).

## GETTING PAST THE FIRST STAGE OF GRIEF: DENIAL

To get past this first stage of grief, denial, you must get to a point where you can accept the tragedy that has befallen you. In the last chapter, you identified what that tragedy is. For Warren, it was the death of his grandfather. In his next session with Warren, Dr. Meier explored that tragedy with him.

"How long has it been? Over twenty years? Yet I find it hard to even say the words," Warren said. "You know, even if he didn't die as they told me he had, he would be nearly ninety by now—he probably would have died of old age."

"Well, that's not necessarily true," Dr. Meier said. "But there was no reason for those people to lie to you back then.

And he wouldn't have left you. Kids instinctively know when they're loved, and your grandfather obviously loved you."

"But my parents left me," Warren said, his tone hesitant and sorrowful.

"But your grandfather didn't. He passed on. Died. It took death to separate him from you. Nothing else could."

Just hearing it put that way had the effect of buoying Warren. He straightened ever so slightly, tears of joy in his eyes.

"Okay," Dr. Meier began again, "It's time for you to work through this. The first thing I want you to do is say out loud, 'My grandpa is dead.'"

"Really?" Warren choked slightly. "You want me to say that?"

"You know it's the truth. In your heart of hearts. So now is the time to admit it."

Warren hesitated but finally found the words. "My grandpa is dead." His hand suddenly went to his chest and his breathing became labored. "I can't believe I said that. All my life, since he left—since he died—I've said things like that. 'Since he left,' and, 'they said he died.' That's the first time I've ever put those words together."

## SAY WHAT YOU'VE BEEN UNABLE TO SAY

You need to do what Warren did. Out loud, now, say the words you have been unable to say all this time, those words that state unequivocally the tragedy that has befallen you.

"The next thing we need to identify," Dr. Meier told Warren, "is the reason saying that in the first place was so difficult."

"He loved me," Warren said, the three words packed with sadness.

"And what did his death do to you?"

At first Warren shrugged, unable or unwilling to attempt to

answer the question. After a little exploration by Dr. Meier he finally said, "Because he was the only one who loved me, and probably no one else ever would."

"Can you see how devastating that message was, and still is, to you—how devastating it would have been to anyone?"

Warren nodded, the realization quite painful.

Now, you do the same thing Warren did. State in very plain and unambiguous terms why it was difficult to admit that the tragedy occurred in the first place. It could be the same answer Warren gave: he thought no one loved him and no one ever would. Perhaps your answer is different—the reality of the tragedy makes you terribly vulnerable, or produces a fear, or means that those closest to you mean you harm. Only you know what that statement is. And only you can state it. So state it right now. And, as before, state it clearly and understandably.

Between sessions Dr. Meier asked Warren to write a good-bye letter to his dead grandfather and actually place it on his grave, to be sure no denial was left in place.

At the next session Dr. Meier said, "The next thing we have to do is to show you how untrue your no-one-ever-loved-me statement is, to show that you *were* loved and that people have loved you since."

"But it is true," Warren protested.

"Well, let's first define what love is. What do you think it is, Warren?"

"What God says it is—when you do good for the person, when you sacrifice for them and make sure they're taken care of. You care about what is best for someone else."

"Okay. Let's go with that."

In the next few minutes Dr. Meier had Warren list all the people who had been good to him over the years, people who had helped and sacrificed for him. They included the people in whose homes he had stayed while he was growing up, teachers who had helped and gone out of their way for him, and youth leaders at church. He ended up with ten names on the list.

"Now, it's true that your mother and father did not do right by you. No one is denying that. You have to accept that. But others did. And here's the list of them. You were loved, Warren."

He stared at the list for a few long moments. "Yes, I guess I was."

## DEBUNK THE MESSAGE OF THE TRAGEDY

Dr. Meier helped Warren show that the statement, "I was never loved," was not true. Now it's time for you to accomplish the same thing—to debunk the statement playing on your internal tape. If there are a few messages involved, write down why each of them is a lie or not as true as you have made it out to be. For instance, write down all the reasons there is no need to fear. Why the threat truly does not exist. As before, be clear and concise.

Just as Dr. Meier showed Warren that he had been loved, he helped him see that he could and would be loved again.

"There's another message," he pointed out to Warren. "'I'll never be loved again.'"

"I haven't been loved," Warren said. "I don't even date."

"Dating aside, how many people in your adult life have you made the effort to get close to?"

Warren shook his head. "Not many."

"How many women have you asked out?"

"One, about three years ago. She looked at me like I was crazy. That look stunted my dating career."

Dr. Meier smiled. "My wife turned me down for three years before she would even date me. But that aside, God tells us that our main focus should be to love others," he said. "How have you been loving others, Warren?"

"Others?" he repeated. "I'm not doing much of that at all."

"And a lot of that is due to your depression. Depressions cause us to look inward, which means that we're not looking around for people we can help. If you're looking to be loved, the fastest way to get there is to love others."

Warren grinned. "I know what comes now. Take a pencil and paper and list as many ways as I can how I could be loving others, then pick a few and get busy. Right?"

"You got it. And don't be general. 'Give my old clothes to the Salvation Army' is not what I'm looking for. Be specific—name a real person. 'Help Mrs. O'Leary with her cow.' That's what I mean. Now, doing this will do two things. It will help you get that love you crave. But it will also begin to build a support group of people who care about you and people whom you can trust."

When Warren had struggled for a while over the list, Dr. Meier stopped him. "You can finish that at home and bring the list with you next time. Now I want to bring up something else—or rather someone else. God. The true solution to this issue of being loved is to really believe God loves you—so that you're gathering your strength and well-being from Him.

"I want you to find some Bible verses that affirm the fact that God loves you and wants the best for you. Then I want you to put them on little cards and carry them with you. When you find those destructive tapes playing in your head, telling you you're alone and will always be alone, I want you to do two things: read the list of people who have loved you over the years and read the verses that affirm God's love for you.

Dr. Meier gave Warren a few verses to get him started. "For example, 1 John 4:16 says, 'And so we know and rely on the love God has for us. God is love. Whoever lives in love lives in God, and God in him" (NIV). Then read the whole chapter of Psalm 139—one of the best! Remember, Warren, what I told you earlier about the fact that we all tend to think God is like our earthly father or mother."

## *AFFIRM WHAT BRINGS YOU COMFORT*

Now, you do the same. Put down on paper all the reasons the tragedy has not caused all the things you feared it would. Also, find and write down on little cards—memorize them as time goes on—as many verses as you can find that affirm what you need affirmed. If, like Warren, you feel unloved, find and use the verses that assure you you are loved. If you have lived in fear, write down the ones that assure you you have nothing to fear (Psalm 91 is a good one), and so on.

---

### Working Through Denial

What follows is a recap of the five steps that will help you work your way through the denial stage of grief. Doing these steps may take some time. It will definitely take some emotional energy. But it is essential you take the time and expend the energy.

1. Identify verbally and in writing the tragedy you have been denying. For Warren, it was saying, "My grandfather is dead," and then writing his grandpa a letter.

2. Identify verbally and in writing why it was difficult to accept the tragedy in the first place. It could be a true reason or a false belief, like Warren's: "It meant I was no longer loved and would never be loved again."

3. Show clearly how the reason you found accepting the tragedy is false. For Warren, it was the list of people who had loved him throughout the years.

---

4. Begin the process of looking outside yourself to bring love and comfort to others and build a support group for yourself. For example, Warren listed those things he could do to love others.

5. Write down on small cards the Bible verses that comfort you and reaffirm that what the tragedy originally meant to you was false—or that you can survive it, even if true. Then work through those cards each time you hear the old internal tape playing.

Then, when that distressful tape is running in your head, take out the cards and work through them. Never forget, God is right there with you and He has no intention of allowing you to call on Him and not be comforted. Reprogram your brain's "computer." In psychiatry, we call this cognitive restructuring. In lay terminology, it's called positive (but realistic) thinking.

The next stage of grief is anger directed outward. If you have just worked your way through the first stage, denial, your goal is now to minimize the anger that may be coming up. In Don's case, though, the goal was a little different.

## GETTING PAST THE SECOND STAGE OF GRIEF: ANGER DIRECTED OUTWARD

It took Don two more sessions to finally admit, "I was mad at Mom, so mad I couldn't see straight. Here I was, I'd graduated from high school a year early. I was even taking some of my first-year college courses at the local J.C. I had professors talking about full scholarships. And Mom was saying that she needed me to work full-time. I had to work. My family was literally starving.

"Mom was a waitress, there was the mortgage and four kids, and I ate like a horse. We basically lived on her tips. She could have sold our rather large home and moved to a less expensive place, but the old home was sentimental to her. She worked long, grueling hours, and she needed help. I was the only one old enough to give it. But I had such a future opening up for me. The sky was literally the limit."

Dr. Meier watched as the argument went back and forth. "So she had a choice between her sentimental attachment to a house or your future, and she chose the house. What did you choose? You had a choice regardless of hers."

"I went to work. I guess I left home to spite her. She wanted me to find a job close to home, naturally, but I heard about a reasonably high-paying job laying roads on the Navajo reservation, and I took it. I sent her everything but what I needed to live. And I stayed away."

"So you made her pay for choosing the house over you by losing her oldest son."

"Sweet revenge."

"And you felt guilty."

Don nodded. "Revenge isn't all that sweet."

Dr. Meier smiled. "So you admit you were angry at her?"

"I'm not proud to say it. But I was. Very angry. I buried it, though. I guess I'm still pretty hacked off at her."

## ADMIT YOUR ANGER

If you're trapped in stage two because you're not willing to admit you're angry at someone who doesn't seem to deserve your anger, it's time's to come out with it. Say so. Out loud, and with pen and ink. Write, "I am angry at _____." And state the reason why.

For Don the sentence looked like this. "I am angry at my mother because she forced me to go out and work and delayed my bright future, when she could have moved to a less expensive place." Perhaps you're angry at someone who has died—a mother you were never able to get close to, a child who may have caused his or her own death either by carelessness or suicide, a spouse who left you without life insurance. These are not rational feelings, but they are normal, powerful feelings, and they need to be out there where you can deal with them. So get the anger out. Writing it down or saying it out loud to an empty chair are powerful gestalt techniques that literally "suck out" your repressed emotions, helping you to weep and properly grieve. Try it. Let it out!

## PUT THE TRAGEDY IN A DIVINE PERSPECTIVE

In no way are we trying to minimize the tragedy you have suffered, but you must realize that tragedies happen to everyone. Life is difficult. In a real sense, tragedy is a part of life. Tragedies are to be endured, and we're to learn all we can from them, and then move forward. Few tragedies, however severe and emotionally devastating, take away those things which are most important to us—our lives and our mission before God. After a tragedy, in fact, we may have an entirely new mission. And God's love for us never ceases. Within that love we find the strength to endure, and the comfort and solace that only God can give.

When Don saw his future evaporating, he got angry at his mother for delaying his plans. But God had plans for Don (see Eph. 1:11). One of those plans was to meet Melinda, and another was to go to college—both in God's own time, for Don's good. So, the first step to dealing with anger is to realize that what has happened is part of God's permissive plan for you, and He is a loving, comforting God who works only for your good (2 Cor. 1:3–4, Rom. 8:28).

One of the things that helped Don get over his anger was the realization that he had acted selfishly too—his mother's "sins" were his as well. Now, that's not to say that a mother working very hard to feed her family is selfish in asking a healthy son to take a job and help out. But in Don's mind, the same "mind" that caused his anger and jealousy toward Melinda, his mother was being terribly selfish by not selling their large house.

"And I was no better," Don said, his remorse evident. "Depriving her of her oldest son was very, very selfish. I need to tell her that. We don't talk much now. I think that's going to change, and the first thing I'm going to tell her is how selfish I was."

When we realize that we have sinned in the same way, and our Heavenly Father, the one we have sinned against, is not angry at us because of our failing, then we have no reason to be angry at someone else because of his or her failing. Don forgave his mother and asked God to forgive him for his chronic bitterness toward her.

## FORGIVENESS

Often our anger is a silent call for vengeance. Don actually exercised a form of revenge on his mother by moving away. If she was going to ask him to work, he was going to deprive her of his company.

As Don found out, revenge was not as sweet as he had expected. When we are not in a position to extract vengeance, or when we believe our anger is unjustified, our anger goes "underground" and becomes depression. Christians are especially vulnerable to suppressed anger. If that's true for you, you need to forgive. Let it go and turn the problem over to the Lord. God proclaims, "Vengeance is mine; I will repay, saith the Lord" (Rom. 12:19 KJV). When we forgive, we are literally making God our Holy Hitman. We are giving up our anger and asking the Lord to take care of it. Of course, we then have to abide by whatever the Lord does.

We had a client once who was extremely angry at a neighbor who had a habit of tossing trash into our client's backyard. Our client spent all summer trying to work up forgiveness for the individual. Finally, when the trees were turning golden, she managed. "Lord, he's all yours," she said with a certain pride. Not three weeks later the man came to know the Lord at a local church. Our client suddenly had a whole new sin to repent of—anger at the Lord for rewarding the trash-thrower with eternal life!

### Working Through Anger Directed Outward

Just to place the steps in a neat bundle, here's a recap of the steps to work your way through the second stage of grief, anger directed outward.

1. Admit your anger, if you have some—no matter how selfish that anger might sound.

2. Put the tragedy in divine perspective. No matter how devastating the tragedy, God still has a life of service and love for you. He will take you home when He is finished loving people through you here on earth.

3. Understand that you're a sinner too. We all are. God is willing to forgive any sin, if we repent and confess it to Him.

4. Forgive. Let it go, give it over to the Lord, and get on with your life. And if you've already taken out a little vengeance, seek God's forgiveness. Make amends where it would be appropriate.

5. Do good to the target of your anger. Do your best

to make things as they should be through prayer and/or appropriate action. The Bible says that if we are kind to our enemies, we actually heap coals of fire on their heads (Prov. 25:22).

6. Begin to work through the next stage: anger directed inward.

Don revealed in a counseling session that he was going to call his mother and reestablish their relationship. The final step in dealing with anger is reestablishing an appropriate relationship with the target of your anger—unless it is a person who is dangerous physically or emotionally. Some broken relationships should stay that way. But that doesn't keep you from praying for the person. In any case, you now want to get things back to where they should be, so do everything reasonable to accomplish that.

## GETTING PAST THE THIRD STAGE OF GRIEF: ANGER DIRECTED INWARD

Melinda is suffering from a major depression. It would be silly to believe that just by reading a few paragraphs in a book she would suddenly shed her depression and rejoin the land of the happy and contented. But it is not silly to believe that she would be able to learn the steps to take and over a number of weeks, perhaps months, with the help of a Christian counseling professional, she would be able to work through them, one by one, and find herself well on the way to recovery.

If you are dealing with major depression, the same is true for you. The typical patient at one of our clinics needs about fifty hours of counseling to dissolve a major depression. But some need less. And some need years to overcome severe childhood abuse. We give you this statistic so that your expectations might be at the right level.

That said, let's help Melinda, and you, take the next step to wellness by working your way through this stage—anger directed inward—and on to an honest expression of grief.

## VOICE YOUR ANGER AT YOURSELF

As with working your way through the other stages, the work here begins the same way: voice your anger at yourself. Tell yourself why you feel so guilty. What is it you did? Melinda had a litany of things. She thought she had gotten angry at Don when he hadn't deserved it. In reality, Don had transferred his maternal anger toward her, then Melinda felt totally rejected because of her own childhood. A lack of insight contributed to Don's depression as well as Melinda's.

She erroneously thought she had been a horrible wife and now she was a horrible mother. Perhaps she had not been sensitive enough to the stress he was under at work? Or to the stress he was under trying to provide for the family?

All her questions produced a lot of guilt, mostly false guilt, and a lot of anger directed toward herself. She already had a ton of childhood shame that she carried throughout life.

So Dr. Meier asked Melinda to write down all the reasons for her guilt. When she was done, she handed him the list. He read it and said, "Now let's work on getting rid of all this."

"Why get rid of it?" she groaned. "I deserve it."

"As I read this," Dr. Meier began, "it occurs to me that these feelings of yours did not occur in a vacuum. Don did something first that caused you to react the way you did."

"Well, yes. I guess he did."

"In fact, he said he was jealous of you—maybe said some things he shouldn't have."

"I know. But he was under a lot of stress at work . . ."

"But maybe you were reacting in a reasonable way. Why don't you list all the things he did and said that gave you the impression there was a problem you needed to react to."

The first step in dealing with self-anger—guilt, shame—is to understand what precipitated the upheaval in the first place. This could take some courage. You may be dealing with tragic events, perhaps the death of a child or a parent, a death for which you feel partially responsible. But that's okay. You need to explore your feelings surrounding that event. What led up to the tragedy—who decided what? Who did and said what? And why?

Now, just as Dr. Meier took a moment to study Melinda's list, study your own.

"I see here," Dr. Meier noted, "That you worked pretty hard to look good for him and Don ignored your efforts—even said something that was unkind."

"Yes, he did."

"That wasn't very nice," Dr. Meier said. "I know my wife would be pretty hurt if I did that to her. In fact, it might lead to a real battle. Husbands need to be sensitive to their wives' needs, regardless of what's going on at work."

"Really?" Melinda said, and she straightened perceptibly.

As you go down your list, be objective in assigning responsibility. If you are dealing with a real tragedy, one where the recipient of the responsibility might have died, assign it anyway. Like truth, responsibility does not change due to events, no matter how tragic.

When you have finished assigning responsibility to each of the events leading up to the tragedy—in Melinda's case, leading up to the feeling that she was being totally emotionally abandoned, because of her childhood experiences—then look again at the list. Is anything that happened your fault? It could be that a few things are, and we'll deal with those in a second. As for the others, even though we would like to shoulder responsibility for people, it is not right that we do so. God tells us that we are responsible for our own work, and that's the way it should be. From now on, if you feel guilty about anything that appears on the list that was not your fault, dismiss the guilt as inappropriate, no matter how much you want to shield the other person.

For those events that *were* your responsibility, ask yourself if what you did was a mistake—we all make mistakes—or was it the appropriate thing to do and it just turned out badly? One of our clients sent her seventeen-year-old son to the store for milk, and he was killed in an auto accident on the way home. Even though she blamed herself for not going to the store herself, sending him was not inappropriate—it was a natural thing to do. Are things like that on your list? When you begin feeling guilty about those things, just tell yourself—as many times as you need to—that you were only doing what made sense at the time. That's all.

Any events left? Are there mistakes you've made that may be difficult to forgive? Mistakes for which it's easy to feel guilty, easy to find shame? If there are, let's take the next step. I have personally counseled repentant drunk drivers who killed someone (sometimes their own children), repentant adulterers, repentant child molesters, even repentant murderers. God will forgive anyone who sincerely repents.

## Forgive Yourself

"To err is human, to forgive divine."

There is so much wisdom in those seven words. You are human, and humans make mistakes. God made you that way. And He loves you still. Part of His love is forgiving your mistakes and helping you overcome them. If you have made a mistake, even a costly one, the time has come to do the divine thing: ask God to forgive you, then forgive yourself.

First, you pray. Pray for wisdom, for understanding, pray that you might learn what there is to learn, and pray for God to relieve you of your guilt. Jesus paid for every sin by His death on the cross.

Then, if your mistake caused harm to someone with whom you can now make amends, do so. Apologize. Do whatever seems appropriate to undo what you've done.

Next, stop punishing yourself. The God of the universe is not going to, why should you? As Scripture tells us in 1 John 2:12, "I write to you, dear children, because your sins have been forgiven on account of his name" (NIV).

Now, if the tape begins playing in your head again, telling you what a bad person you are, how you've done something terrible and deserve nothing but reproach, tell that voice that you have forgiven yourself, because God has forgiven you first.

---

### Working Through Anger Directed Inward

If you're stuck in the third stage of grief, anger directed inward, work through the steps summarized below.

1. Voice your anger at yourself. State why you feel so guilty.

2. Explore your feelings surrounding the tragedy. What led up to it? Who did and said what? Be objective in assigning responsibility.

3. Is anything that happened your fault? If not, do not assume responsibility for someone else's actions or words.

4. If you were at fault, ask God to forgive you, then forgive yourself. Apologize or make amends where appropriate.

5. Stop punishing yourself.

These are not easy things. As we said before, it may take a while for you to thoroughly work through these steps and gain their benefit. But don't be deterred by the time, energy, or discipline it might require. The steps will work and your diligence will pay off.

And, when it has, you will move on to the fourth stage of grief.

## Getting Past the Fourth Stage: Genuine Grief

In the last chapter, we covered how to work your way through this last stage, the stage of genuine grief. Just to recap, this is where you give yourself permission to cry, to talk about what's on your mind with people who love you, and as you do, to work through the hurt and the loss.

We also hope that by the time you get here, your depression has been decreased by one of the previous steps. It was for Don and Melinda. Although both thought they had something to grieve in the beginning, after working through the stages they found they both had more childhood grieving to do than grieving for the current stresses they were under. Their task then shifted to loving one another again and working on those things that were keeping them from communicating honestly with one another—the issues that got them into trouble in the first place.

Warren, on the other hand, did have something to grieve— or rather someone, the passing of his grandfather those many years before, as well as the abandonment of his parents. When he got to this stage, sitting in the doctor's office, he broke down in deep, cleansing tears. So much had gone on over the years it was impossible to understand all that his tears meant. But when they finally subsided and a few weeks had passed—a few weeks when he allowed himself to relive some of the times he'd had with his grandpa, when he allowed himself some time for closure—he felt the cork slowly slip from his happiness bottle and its joyous contents invade and forever buoy his spirit.

Your road to happiness includes a time of genuine grief too. Now is the time to give yourself permission to experience it. Take all the time and shed all the tears you need. And when your grief is done, come back and keep working.

## THE FIFTH STAGE OF GRIEF: RESOLUTION

This is the only automatic stage of grief. If you have worked your way through the previous four, the fifth—resolution—just happens. And resolution means a return of joy and a zest for life. But perhaps there are residual emotions still swirling around inside you—anger, fear, guilt, loneliness, a fear of abandonment, confusion, worry about loss of control, or any combination of these painful emotions.

Remember, you have just come through a difficult time. What you're feeling is natural, and that's the point. *It's natural.* After an operation there is residual pain. In Part 3, we will present some spiritual principles that will not only help you dissolve that residual pain but help you inoculate yourself against future bouts of depression.

But before we give you the guidelines to happiness and the keys to spiritual renewal, there are two more items we want to deal with briefly, and these are understanding where anger comes from and the role anger plays in moods and mood swings. When you comprehend these, then you can move from anger to the opposite end of the emotional spectrum: happiness.

# 12 UNDERSTANDING ANGER

Happiness and anger are at opposite ends of the emotional spectrum. It is hard to imagine a happy person who spends much time being angry. Happiness is such a light, contented emotion, while anger seethes and boils and frets and plans revenge. And if anger is dealt with improperly, if it is simply swallowed, it will one day boil back up to wreak even greater destruction.

Melinda's depression grew from her anger. There were other emotions at work too: betrayal, a sense of worthlessness, an inability to control the world around her. Even these emotions had their roots in anger—anger at being betrayed, anger at being treated as if she were worthless, anger at the world being wrested away from her. But even then, had she dealt with the anger properly, things could have been very different. Perhaps she and her husband would have had long, meaningful discussions and come away from them more in love and with a greater feeling of emotional safety than ever before.

But they didn't.

And because they didn't, Melinda plunged herself into what seemed to her like an unfathomable, uncontrollable depression. A major depression.

Has anger taken up residence in your life? Perhaps anger is even wrapped up in your moods somehow. But whether it is or not, only good comes when you learn to deal with anger in a godly way. Psychiatrists often say that most environmentally (rather than genetically) caused depressions are merely "anger turned inward." Inappropriate handling of anger is not only the leading cause of depression, it is a leading cause of death, since prolonged anger also lowers our antibodies and resistance to disease.

So here are our suggestions for understanding anger. The first thing we will cover is anger itself—what it is. Then we will go on to discuss where it comes from, and, finally, what to do about it.

## What Anger Is

Anger is, in its simplest definition, a demand for change. Something occurs that you don't like, and anger erupts saying, "Stop it! And never do that again!" The anger can be toward yourself, toward others, or toward God.

Of course, there are other, far less explosive responses when negative things happen. When wronged, we can often simply learn from the incident and go on. Or, when our sense of right is offended, we can take the opportunity to witness—telling the other person why our sense of right is, indeed, right. So anger is not the only reaction we can have to these things. But it is a common reaction.

Anger comes from the most vulnerable part of us. After all, when we are secure in our little corner of the world, an injustice does not mean quite so much. It will pass, or be dealt with by the system, or by God. However, if we are physically or emotionally vulnerable, an injustice can be quite threatening—we could end up losing something dear to us, even our freedom. So anger erupts. Our backs go up like a cat backed into a corner, and we lash out. The apostle Paul gave us permission in Ephesians 4:26 to become angry in a way that is without sin, as Jesus did.

So, since anger is not a stranger to any of us, let's take a closer look at it.

## WHERE ANGER COMES FROM

Some people are angry all the time; anger is as much a part of them as their arms and legs. Their anger came from who knows where, but it came early in their lives and planted deep roots. Anger defines these people as human beings. Anger like that is terribly destructive—it saps energy, relationships, happiness, and, frankly, everything and everyone who makes life worth living.

Now, if you're one of these angry people, stop reading right here and go find yourself a good Christian counselor and get some serious help. You and everyone else will thank God you did for a long time thereafter.

For most of us, though, anger boils up intermittently from somewhere inside us as a result of something that occurs outside us. So let's take a look at what some of those things that trigger anger are.

### ANGER CAN BE PERSONAL

To be angry about something, you have to care about it. Melinda cared deeply about her husband, Don, and the depth of his love. How he felt about her was easily the most important thing in her life. So the signals that he no longer cared wounded her severely and presented her emotional world with quite an earthquake.

Had the mailman decided to feel negatively toward her, or the florist down the street, she would not have cared all that much. The less you care about something, the less likely you will get angry about it.

That stands to reason. So it also stands to reason that since we all care about different things for different reasons, anger can erupt in one person because of a particular event, but not in another. Two men, for example, can watch the same football game and react in opposite ways. One is a die-hard fan, someone whose whole identity is wrapped up in the success of his favorite team. Another is a casual watcher, one who enjoys the game for the game's sake and has only a passing interest in who wins or loses. When the home team blows a game-winning field goal in the last seconds of the game, the die-hard explodes in a tirade. The casual fan simply slaps him on the back and says, "We'll get 'em next time."

In much the same way, Melinda was surprised at what one of the other ladies said the night of the company Christmas party, when she was still reeling from her husband's perceived indifference. Melinda had been left alone while Don went to speak with friends. She complained to the other woman at the table that her husband was not paying the proper attention to her. "They never do," the woman said, with a dismissive wave of the hand. "Men just don't understand how we women think. It's no big deal. Don't worry about it." Since Don's indifference proclaimed to Melinda that his love toward her was cooling, how could anyone tell her not to worry about it? In Melinda's mind, it was the only thing worth worrying about.

So, when anger comes, take a moment to identify what it is you care about that is providing the anger's heat. It might be easy to identify, like Melinda's, or it might be more difficult. But by identifying it you will better understand your anger and what is fueling it, and then you will be in a better position to deal with it. For instance, Melinda could have gone to her husband and simply said, "When you treat me with this kind of indifference, it tells me you don't love me like you used to. Do you love me less?" It's a gutsy thing for a woman to ask, but at least her husband would then have the opportunity to respond, setting the record straight one way or the other.

Knowing what is fueling the anger also helps us deal more lovingly with others. If you know, for instance, that your father is quite particular about his grass—he cuts and trims it twice a week and can't stand footprints across it after it's been newly cut—you would probably want to avoid walking across the lawn when you come to visit. Granted, his love for his grass might be a little off-center, but there's still no reason to provoke a confrontation.

But sometimes the smallest of things can provoke an angry outburst.

## LITTLE THINGS CAN PROVOKE A BIG REACTION

Brenda found this to be true when Dr. Minirth helped her analyze her own behavior. On those days when she felt irritable and had the electric current of depression running through her, if one of the kids spilled milk, or another scattered books all over the kitchen floor, she would react as if they had murdered someone. She would be all over them. Or if she had just gotten through mopping the floor and her husband walked in with even the smallest speck of mud on his shoes, he might as well have been caught in a bar with a bimbo. That's how Brenda reacted—completely out of proportion.

Anger can, and often does, erupt from what appears to be small things.

Why? Small things often represent big things in our minds. On those irritable days, Brenda saw the spilled milk not as just her child having an accident, but as life turning against her. No longer was life a well-ordered, well-greased affair unfolding as it ought, but life had become a living organism bent on thwarting her. She was not as angry at her child as she was her ultimate enemy—what her life had suddenly become and the difficulty she now had dealing with it. Of course, if we take this to its logical conclusion, she is actually angry at the One who orders our lives, allows bad things to happen to good people (the rain falls "on the just and the unjust"), and causes her life to no longer be bearable: God Himself.

Little things can also be the proverbial straw that breaks the camel's back. And we've all had those. We're patient as the child puts on the wrong socks, then gets her dress dirty, then rips her homework papers in half. But when that milk spills—well, that's it. How clumsy can one child be?

When anger does erupt, take a look at what you're angry about and weigh it against those things that are really important— your relationship with your kids, your spouse, your friends, and your God. If it really is a small thing, take some deep breaths, count to ten, walk away and cool off, and come back when you can put things back in perspective. What difference will that spilt milk be a hundred years from now when you are in heaven looking back at that incident?

If anger at small things is a consistent problem, then get into Christian counseling or some other accountability program to help place those small things where they belong in your balanced, Christian life. Perfectionism can cause you to expect too much (such as a child who doesn't spill his milk) and result in too much anger and depression.

## SOME ANGER IS BASED ON SELFISHNESS
Paul Meier sat facing Don and Melinda. "After working with each of you separately for a while, I thought it might be a good idea for us to meet together."

162

"Good," Don said, "it'll be good for us to talk."

Dr. Meier then turned to Melinda. "I know Melinda has something she wants to say to you."

Keeping a smile etched on his face, Don turned toward his wife. Melinda, in turn, studied him for a long moment, then cleared her throat and began. "I know this took place a couple of months ago," she said, "but you started treating me with a lot of indifference. I would get new clothes, work all day getting ready for one of your business dinners—get my hair done, even a make-over once. And when I would present myself, you'd say nothing. Like I didn't even exist. You used to compliment me and say how nice I looked. Then, all of a sudden, it was nothing."

"Is that what all this moping around has been about?" Don said, almost as if he were on the attack.

"Don," Dr. Meier said, "it's best in these situations for you just to respond to the specifics."

Don nodded. "Okay. We're talking about just before you decided to give up on everything?"

Melinda nodded.

Don's eyes darted away suddenly and for a moment he looked as if he were trying to avoid saying something. But he must have decided to come clean, because he took a deep breath and said, "Work suddenly got very difficult back then. It still is."

"In what way?" Dr. Meier asked.

"About the first of the year I lost two very large accounts to the competition. Management told me if I lose another one, I'm on the street."

Melinda's eyes widened. "Why didn't you tell me?"

"I didn't want to worry you."

"It was better to make me think you didn't love me anymore?"

"Don," Dr. Meier interrupted, "there's more here, isn't there?"

"More?" Don responded.

"Yes. More. You knew you were making that trade-off with Melinda, yet you were willing to make it. Why?"

"More," Don said flatly. "I was mad at Melinda."

Dr. Meier pointed a pencil at Melinda. "Tell her."

Don turned his eyes back to his wife. "I was mad at you. I'm not proud of that, but I was."

"At me? Why? What did I do?"

"I was under such pressure at work. Working so hard to make a buck and keep the bills paid and the family going. And you were at home with the kids. The only pressure you had was to make sure you took something out of the freezer for dinner. It just didn't seem fair. I know it was wrong, but suddenly I just could hardly look at you. Then you started going downhill and I started getting madder—and trying to cover it up."

"You were mad at me?"

"Let's take a second here," Dr. Meier said, "and let me explain something to you two."

He pointed out to Don and Melinda that anger often comes from selfishness. Melinda had seen a change in her husband. Instead of trying to find out what was going on in his life that caused it, instead of selflessly putting her own hurts aside to help her husband reveal his own needs and then help him satisfy them, she chose to take everything personally and hold on to her anger instead of verbalizing it.

Don, in turn, chose to put himself and what he was going through ahead of his wife's needs, and as a result, he got angry at her. To Don, she had become an impediment, an anchor keeping him in the pressure cooker rather than the helpmate God had given him—someone who had been there for him in the past and who would be there for him now.

When your anger boils up, look for selfishness. You will find it more often than not. Some anger, like the anger Jesus had, comes from our own righteous indignation at an unjust act. But much of our anger comes from our own selfish demands and expectations.

Anger can also come from our subtle fears and outright paranoia.

## PROJECTING YOUR PARANOIA

In their counseling sessions, Dr. Minirth helped Brenda see that she frequently placed her own paranoia on her husband. As she faced another day of irritability and that constant current of depression, she would look at her husband and just know he was angry at her for putting him through another day of this. It did not matter how he greeted her that morning, she would read anger into it. Why? Because she was treating him so badly that he just had to be angry—what else could he possibly be? The anger was her own, but she was projecting it onto him, like a slide projector (seeing the toothpick in her "brother's" eye rather than the log in her own, as described in Matthew 7:3–5 by Jesus).

If you are angry at someone because he is angry at you, take a hard look at the dynamic. Are you angry just because you think he's mad at you? If so, put the anger aside and work with the other person to mend the underlying issues in the relationship. Don't try to be a mind reader. Go ask him if he is angry. Don't assume it.

## ANGER AT INANIMATE OBJECTS OR ACCIDENTS

Brenda had had a particularly difficult morning. Jake had left about 4:30 A.M. to catch a plane and Brenda had not been able to get back to sleep. To make things easier on herself, she promised pancakes for breakfast if the kids would get ready for school and also make their beds. Then she found she was out of pancake mix. The ensuing battle caused her to be on a very ragged edge as she drove them to school. When she finally stopped the car in front of the big red brick building, the passenger side door would not unlock. No matter what she did, her six-year-old daughter, Hannah, could not get the door open. It was more than she could bear. Brenda threw open her own door and crossed quickly to Hannah's door and began beating on it, screaming at it, and pulling on the outside handle. To her, that door had become a living thing, and it was standing between her and the resumption of life as she knew it.

It seems silly to get angry at things, or accidents, doesn't it? After all, if anger is a demand for change, how could that door, or a chair you stumble over, change? Or how could anger have prevented an accident from happening? But there's not one of us who hasn't been angry at something without its own pulse.

Why? Like Brenda, we feel we're being thwarted and, darn it! We're going to get mad at something—there's just too much negative energy bubbling up not to. And the door—or whatever—is handy.

It's also a lot safer to get angry at a door, or a chair, or a pen that's run out of ink. The door is not going to get angry back or tell you how foolish you are for losing control. Often when we begin cursing things, we're simply taking the easy way out. Instead of dealing with our anger and its human target, we are avoiding the confrontation—until later, when the anger boils up uncontrollably and the confrontation may be far more destructive.

So when you begin throwing things around, take a hard look at the real object of your anger and deal with him or her.

## SOME ANGER IS APPROPRIATE

It's no secret. God created us in His own image, which means that we possess most of God's attributes. He is creative and so are we. He loves. We do too. He gets angry and we do too. He programmed anger into us, and there are times when our anger is quite appropriate. Generally, when we are faced with real wrongdoing, real injustice, or real offenses against our sense of what is right, we are justified in getting angry. The apostle Paul said so in Ephesians 4: "In your anger do not sin: Do not let the sun go down while you are still angry, and do not give the devil a foothold" (vv. 26–27 NIV).

Although we have shown that an element of Melinda's anger was based on selfishness, another element of her anger came from the fact that her husband was treating her wrongly. We are "one flesh" with our husbands or wives. They are commanded to live for us and we are commanded to live for them. When a spouse behaves in a way contrary to that commandment, we are justified in our anger, just as we are justified when we see the weak being bullied by the strong. Or the powerful corrupting the innocent. Or God's law being trampled by an indifferent, self-indulgent society.

So when you begin to analyze your anger, which is always the first step in dealing with it, part of that analysis is to determine if your anger is justified.

Let's summarize what we have discussed up to this point.

When you feel your anger boiling up and threatening to get the better of you, do the following:

1. Since anger can be quite personal, take a look at your emotions and see if you are angry about something that is reasonably important. If it's not—if you're angry at a flea-sized problem, or if your anger seems to be burning more hotly than most people might find appropriate—there is probably an underlying cause with each you need to cope.

2. If what you're angry about is a little thing, decide if it is just the last straw, or if the little thing represents

something far larger in your mind. In either case, put it all in proper perspective. See the little thing in light of the damage your anger may be doing to far more important things, like your family relationships. Then calm down.

3. Since a lot of anger is based on selfishness, take a hard look at what you're angry about and take the selfishness out of it. If any part of the anger is selfish, then that part of your anger is inappropriate and you need to work your way through it and regain control.

4. If you are angry at someone because of what you think he or she is doing or feeling, then you need to pull back and find out for sure. More often than not you are projecting your own destructive feelings on the other person. Ask. Don't assume and don't try to be a mind reader.

5. Are you directing your anger at an inanimate object? Or an accident? Then pull back and determine what you're really angry at. Your anger might very well be appropriate, but unless the object of the anger is properly identified, you will never deal with it properly.

6. Determine if your anger is appropriate. Take care not to cloak yourself in self-righteousness. But if your anger is directed toward a legitimate wrong, one that God would see as wrong, then in all probability you have a case. Even if your anger is legitimate, however, there is a proper way to deal with it.

Now that you have analyzed your anger—you've determined its origin and identified whether it is appropriate or not—it's time to learn how to properly deal with it. That lesson is one of the guidelines to happiness, which we will look at next.

PART 3

# ACHIEVING
# WHOLENESS
## AND HAPPINESS

# 13 GUIDELINES TO HAPPINESS

Whether your moods and mood swings have origins in emotional or genetic issues, it is important that you lay a good foundation upon which to build what we all want for our lives: happiness—a sense of joy, of well-being, and contentment. By laying this foundation first, those elements of your depression and other moods that are aggravated simply by the way you approach life will dissolve. And when they do, what will be left are those issues we need to deal with more proactively.

What we're going to discuss in this chapter are practical guidelines to living a happier, more fulfilled life. As with any set of instructions, they are more easily put down on paper and read than they are put into practice. Rest assured, we understand that. But that said, we still want to urge you to make the effort and establish the discipline necessary to make these guidelines a reality for you. Your life will become a real force for the Lord as well as much happier and more fulfilled when you do. These same guidelines have helped hundreds of thousands of people for over twenty years now.

As you might guess, Melinda had misgivings about such a process and voiced them when she met with Dr. Meier.

"Guidelines to happiness?" Melinda commented after he told her about them. "Wouldn't a ticket to Disney World be easier?" Melinda slouched in her chair, her eyes at half-mast. "Anyway, it's all a waste of time. I don't have the energy to be happy."

Paul Meier smiled. "The tragedy is that you're probably right. But we're going to get you that energy. Two things happen when you're more satisfied with life, when you're happier. Your serotonin level goes up, which helps eliminate depression. And if you will exercise only twenty minutes at least three days a week, that will produce endorphins, which are another shot in the happiness arm. So by putting a plan in place to make your life more satisfying, we're going to clear the cobwebs out and allow the light to better illuminate those areas of your life that need more direct help."

"But if I can't even get up in the morning, how am I going to do all this other stuff?"

"Melinda, let me be direct. You've been coming here faithfully twice a week now for nearly a month. For you to expend that much effort, you must want to get better. I don't think you like what's happening to you. So even though you talk about an unwillingness to do something, I think that hides some fear. You want to get better, but you want to be led along the path a little bit. Well, I'm willing to do that, if you're willing to travel that path one step at a time. Are you willing?"

Melinda thought for a moment. Then her head began to nod. "Okay. Make me happy?"

Paul laughed softly. He liked Melinda. Even though she was going through a difficult situation, one that had left her emotionally bruised, there was still a fire inside of her that now and again revealed itself in little comments like that one. "I can't make anyone but myself happy. But I can be a mirror to you, reflecting what I see in your personal dynamics. I know what works and doesn't work to turn depression into happiness. But you have to do the work. I can only be your coach and cheerleader. I'm pulling for you."

## GUIDELINE 1
## MAKE TIME FOR WORK AND PLAY

"The first thing I want you to do is order your day, making sure you have enough time to do the things you have to do and also enough time to do something you really enjoy—time to play, if you will."

"So I have to go back to work?" she groaned. "I knew there would be a hitch to this."

"But you're going to do it a little differently. You're going to allow time to play. What do you really enjoy doing?"

"Not working."

"I don't believe that. I think you get a lot of satisfaction from being active, doing things, being productive. But we'll tackle that next. What do you enjoy? You used to read, as I recall, do crafts. Do you enjoy doing those things? Or are there other things you enjoy?"

Melinda straightened a little in her chair. Obviously, just thinking about doing those things again was having a strengthening effect. "I do like to do those things. I haven't read a good book in so long. I just haven't had the inclination. But what I'd really like to do is paint. I did some of that back in Gallup."

"So you want to paint."

"Right."

"Okay. Let's take a few minutes—" Dr. Meier handed her a tablet and a pen. "And on this tablet write down all the things you have to do on a normal day."

Having been brought back to reality, Melinda sighed, but she balanced the tablet on her knee and began writing. As with any homemaker, Melinda knew in great detail everything she had to do on a normal day—from getting lunches for the kids to dropping off the dry cleaning to doing the laundry. It was at least five minutes before her head came up. "What now?"

"Can you put any of them in priority? Or are they just a list where everything needs to get done?"

"It all has to get done. That's what is driving the family nuts. I haven't been doing them—well, not all of them. And most of these need to get done either every day or most days."

"Now, how much time would you need daily to paint. To take a class and make progress on a project?"

Melinda looked at Dr. Meier for a long moment. Then she just shook her head. "This isn't going to work. How can I possibly take time away from my family to do something like that?"

"Easy. You're just going to do it. You need time to do something you enjoy—as long as you're getting the other things done. So how much time do you need?"

Melinda suggested a half hour a day, and Dr. Meier doubled it to an hour.

## MAKE YOUR OWN LIST

Fundamental to happiness is that we fulfill our obligations; we behave responsibly and honorably. Why? Because, first, there's a high degree of satisfaction in a job well done, even if it's a job we're not all that enthused about. Second, we avoid the weight of guilt that surrounds failure to do our job. Those two combine to make our emotional and spiritual load lighter.

So let's take a moment and go through the steps you take to fulfilling those obligations. First, write down a list of things you're obligated to do over a given day, a given week; then, if appropriate, prioritize it. Don't leave anything out, even if you think you've slithered out of doing it through neglect. This is the list of things you would do to assuage all guilt and tension and to make sure you're contributing as you ought to those who are counting on you.

After doing this, it is probably a good idea to make an attitude check. As we have discussed, depression sometimes comes from the feeling that we have lost control of our own lives, that we're doing and doing and getting nothing for it. As you look at the list you've just compiled, there are probably a number of things on there you just don't want to do. In fact, just by contemplating them you see your depression deepening.

Now is the time to tell yourself that everything you do is for the Lord. Everything. All the lunches you make for the kids, all the vacuuming and dusting, all the bed-making and picking up, all the meaningless reports you might do for management, all the silly busy-work at school, everything is done for the Lord. So do it well, and with a glad heart. You'll quickly find that with the right attitude, doing even the most unfulfilling job joyfully is not all that hard. After all, God is not an evil taskmaster. On the contrary, He rewards His people, even when they're asked to do the mundane and the miserable. And Jesus said that His yoke is easy, His burden is light.

If you have too many things on your list, they're probably not from God. They may be from your earthly father rather than your Heavenly Father. Were you expected to do too much as a child? Cut the list and delegate a few items. You must have margins in your life. This means time each day when everything on your list is done and you have nothing scheduled at all—some leisure time to regroup. No margin means there are still too many chores on your list, so cut it even more. Figure out a way to do it. You have to.

So, after you've finished the list, take a moment and review it. Are you taking too much on yourself? People do. Homemakers can try to do everything—kids, house, taking care of husband. Husbands can take on too much at work and still try to be everything to everyone at home. Make sure that everyone in the family is pulling their weight. Even little kids can have chores, and as they get bigger and stronger, the chores can grow to match. Also, husbands can be asked to help around the house—taking out the garbage, doing the vacuuming, cleaning up after pets—whatever the two of you agree upon. It's important that our families share responsibilities for the home and for each other. So cut the list more if necessary. Be sure you are able to go to bed early enough every night to wake up naturally, before the alarm clock goes off. Lack of sleep depletes serotonin, causing depression. So living a balanced life also means getting enough sleep, relaxation, exercise, fun, and fellowship.

Well, now you have a task list and you may have no energy left to do it. All your energy was buried in depression. It's important, no matter how difficult it is to get the energy together at first, that you faithfully do the things on that list. As you fulfill your obligations, as the sense of a job well done grows, the energy will grow too. Why? Because doing something well produces the adrenaline to do more, and the satisfaction produces the brain amines that help erase depression.

## MAKE TIME FOR FUN
Just as you made a list of things you have to do, now make a list of things you enjoy. And the list should have two columns on it—things you can do in a half hour to an hour during the day, and things that might be considered field trips—like experiencing a field of wildflowers or going to a ball game.

The next thing you do, and you do it starting on the very first day you begin ticking things off your to-do list, is set time aside—preferably a half hour to an hour—to do something extra on your "fun" list.

Strangely enough, determining what should go on that list might be difficult. Often when we're depressed, we no longer enjoy the things we used to enjoy. Melinda used to read a lot, for example. When depressed, she didn't. Or maybe we've never really allowed ourselves to do something fun just for ourselves. This could be one of the reasons depression gained a foothold in the first place. So let's take a look at some good ways to get some entries on that list.

One way you might start is by asking yourself this question: If you had all the time and money in the world, what would you do for fun? Would you travel? Or paint? Or exercise, or cook, or sit in a hammock and read? What? Then write down the possibilities. Of course, any list that starts out with a question like that probably has some entries on it that lack reality. So take a moment and review the list and bring reality to it. But don't be too hard on yourself. Even if you wrote: "travel to Europe and tour all the castles," there may be feasible things you can do that are related—going to museums, for instance, or looking at travel videos.

Just like the task list, your list of fun things does you no good until you actually do some of the things you've written down. You would think that such an admonition would be unnecessary, that the moment we're given permission to do enjoyable things, we would go out and start doing them. Actually, many of us believe we just don't deserve to do the things we enjoy—as if there's something sinful or selfish in doing them. Nothing could be further from the truth. Jesus came to earth so we could experience an abundant life. God has given you things you enjoy—He has given you talent, interests, and a drive to use them. Not to do so is slighting yourself and God. So enjoy. Whatever the activity, allow yourself to get into it, to lose yourself in it, to refresh yourself while doing it. In short, use this time to recharge your batteries and to bring something to your life that may be missing. So your first priority is to bring balance, margin, and some fun into your life.

## GUIDELINE 2
## DEVELOP FAMILY RELATIONSHIPS

The longer Brenda found herself dealing with her moods and mood swings, the farther her family got from her. Not only did they not want to get caught up in her moods, but she began to turn increasingly inward as she tried to deal with those moods—which is what she saw as the real problem. You might find yourself in the same situation, being farthest from those whom God has placed the closest to you. That is not good. There are a lot of advantages to a strong, close family, not least of which is that the family, by definition, is our physical and emotional support group. They are the ones God has bound by duty to help you out, just as you are duty-bound to help them out. Family members know you and where you came from better than anyone else. And that is powerful knowledge—they know what kind of support you need and how best to deliver it. And one of those things they're best able to deliver is "tough love," that love that may hurt at first but in the long run gets you back on the right track.

Just as taking the necessary steps to build strong family relationships helps direct support your way, it also takes your attention away from yourself and directs it toward others. When you're talking to your parents, or your brothers and sisters, or doing something supportive for your husband and children, you are not thinking about yourself or your problems.

And as you direct your attention to their needs, you will become involved in their problems. You will be listening to them, praying for them, perhaps giving them advice or helping them out. Again, you will be looking outward to those you love rather than inward. And as you help them out you will be getting more good feelings, and the accompanying satisfaction—and more brain amines to ward off future depressions.

But not only are you building strong family ties to help you now, you are building relationships that can weather future storms, as well. No matter how hard you work to eradicate your moods and mood swings, you are going to slip now and again. When you do, you might end up offending a family member or treating one or more of them badly. By taking the time and energy to build a strong relationship now, one that is built on the expectation that there might be a slip or two sometime in the future, when they occur, the relationships will be strong enough to not only survive, but give you the support you need while you're going through your difficult time.

Since Brenda could see her moods and mood swings causing family rifts, she took this guideline seriously. Under Dr. Minirth's guidance, she began to identify her relationships. On a tablet of paper she wrote down the names of all the members of her immediate family: her husband (Jake), the three children, her parents, her two brothers and her sister and their spouses, Jake's parents and his brother and his wife, an aunt and uncle who lived nearby, and her single living grandparent. But she made it more than just a list. Placing each name as a heading, and giving each relation a half-page, Brenda gave herself room to answer some questions about each person—including her husband and kids—and the way she was looking at the relationship. These are the questions she was instructed to ask about each relationship:

- Characterize your current relationship with this person. Is it close, not so close? How often do you see this person? And when you do is the meeting warm, or cordial, marked with tension or indifference, trusting? Is there a lot of laughing, a lot of connecting? Do you empathize with one another? Or are you basically just in the same room? Do the good feelings last beyond the meeting? Do you talk to each other on the phone? Or over e-mail? Be as honest about the relationship as you can, and particularly about any tension or sore spots you may need to deal with or smooth over.

- Is there anything about this person that makes a relationship difficult? This could be just about anything that has stood in the way of a meaningful relationship in the past. Perhaps they are always negative, or indifferent, or abuse alcohol or other substances, or have a real difficulty with anger—particularly at you. Maybe they have character flaws you can't ignore. Any number of things separate us from people over which we have no control. This does not mean you give up on those who have such problems, but it also means you don't build your support group around a relationship with them.

- What are this person's likes and dislikes? When you call him up that first time, it's a good idea to have something to talk about. If your brother likes golf, you can ask him when he played last. If your mom has a vegetable garden, you can ask her how things are growing. Not only will it give you something to talk about, but it will show them that you're interested in what interests them. By knowing what they dislike, you'll know what subjects to avoid.

- What do you have in common with this person? Although this may not be this person's favorite thing, it will be something he or she likes. You brother may play golf, something you don't, but he may also enjoy cooking, something you do. It gives you something to have a conversation about.

- Phone number? Address? E-mail address?

Take time to make your own relationship inventory, just as Brenda did.

Now, once you have answered all these questions, begin building or rebuilding that relationship. And how do you do that? The first thing you do is repair any rough spots in your current relationship. Apologize, if you need to, and seek forgiveness. Then begin doing the things that are appropriate to your relationship. With a spouse or child, begin being a good spouse and parent. Spend time with them, talk to them, listen to them, help them, fulfill your obligations to them—love them. In the case of your siblings, call them. Get to know what's happening in their lives, listen and help when you can. There is no magic in any of this, it is just being a loving sister or brother, and being willing to work at it over the long haul. As time goes on, you will find that reinforcing your relationships will become easier—you'll know enough about each member of your family to know how to maintain your relationship with them. But until then, you have to take the time and energy with each to construct something meaningful.

## GUIDELINE 3
## BUILD FRIENDSHIPS

Next to family, and sometimes in place of family, the best support group is your friends. As we discussed in Chapter 4, moods and mood swings tend to drive wedges between the sufferer and his or her friends. Not only does the sufferer turn her eyes inward and away from friends, but friends often become the victims of the sufferer's moods and mood swings. Since they are not family and are not duty-bound to remain, they may drift away and make new friends elsewhere. The sufferer then finds himself or herself friendship-poor.

So what do you do?

Wendy asked herself that same question. She knew that a

teaching career depends on close, trusting relationships with friends and associates, so she had to solve that problem. And it was a problem. With the advent of Ms. Chimp, that part of her that shows up every other month or so and takes her on a roller coaster ride of wild highs, her relationships had been souring. Of particular concern to her was Ginny, who broke off their friendship after Wendy had let her down in a most callous way. She really couldn't blame Ginny at all. How many others had she offended without even knowing it? Wendy decided it was time to make a concerted effort to build and maintain friendships.

Of course, friendships are very different from family ties. Where a brother is always a brother, a friend is only a friend when he wants to be. So the emphasis on gaining and maintaining friendships is to make sure your friendship is always a positive experience for your friend.

We have already covered some of this ground in the discussion on building and maintaining family relationships, but we will cover it again to emphasize how important it is. The first thing you must do is to inventory your current and potential friends. Write down their names, one on every half-sheet, leaving room to answer questions about them. Although this sounds familiar, there is a difference: who do you put on the list? Unlike relatives, there is no obvious way to identify a friend or potential friend. Sometimes friendship is just based on one thing—a passion for golf, or a particular ministry—and there may be very little in common otherwise. However, in our experience, friends possess other characteristics as well. What follows is a reasonable list of them.

- You sense, at least, a preliminary connectedness between you.

- There is something in common between you upon which you can build a relationship.

- You have complementary personalities.

- There are no character flaws that preclude a supportive relationship.

- There is a sense of empathy with one another.

- Most important, you and that friend can be honest with each other, confess to each other, and pray for each other about any thought, motive, or secret behavior.

There may be other characteristics that you particularly want, and that's fine. After all, they are going to be your friends and you, above all, need to be comfortable with them.

With these characteristics as a guideline, there will not be all that many people who qualify. As you probably already know, friendship—real friendship—is not normally shared between an individual and a lot of other people. Granted, we usually have a number of acquaintances, but not all that many true friends. And that's okay. The idea is, though, that those who are friends are cultivated, treated, and maintained as friends.

So how do you do that?

The first thing you do is spend time with them individually. Go to ball games, rose shows, home shows, out to dinner, over to your house, church functions, Promise Keepers, women's retreats—all those things friends do together. And don't just sit there, share these events with them—the ideas, the excitement, the work—so that the commonality of the events can become a part of each of you and part of your folklore together. Then as time goes on, you will have even more to talk about as shared experience.

And as you share all this time and experience, talk and listen to your friend. This is something Wendy worked hard on, especially when she found herself in her hypomanic phase.

Granted, when that occurred she tried to isolate herself as best she could, but there were still things she was called upon to do. And if while doing one of those she came in contact with another person, she concentrated on listening to what that person had to say and how to respond. But even when you're not in a mood, it's important that you hear what your friends are saying. Not only the words, but the inflection, and sometimes what they're not saying. Get to know your friends—likes, dislikes, the demons they've battled and may still be battling—everything visible and everything floating beneath the surface.

And like any friend, go out of your way for them. Do something special on their birthdays. Help them when they're ill. If you come across something you know they'd like, get it for them (if it's price appropriate). Pray for them. And if they're going through a particularly difficult time at work or home, along with any emotional support you give, pray with them.

Which brings up the need to also be a godly friend. Just as you would want a friend to intervene if you made a wrong decision and found yourself doing sinful things, it's important that you do the same for them. If we see our brother or sister in sin, we are to gently admonish them and win them back to the straight and narrow. This element of friendship becomes more effective, of course, if you have taken the time and energy to build a strong, giving, loving relationship with them beforehand.

And if your friend is not a Christian, then you need to share the Lord with him or her. In fact, your relationship should have this as a primary goal—not only to share the words of the gospel, but your life witness, as well, making sure your words and deeds always glorify God. Of course, there is a danger in these kinds of friendships. You always have to guard against becoming unequally yoked and tainted by the ways of the world your non-Christian friends may bring with them. While we have non-Christian friends, our most intimate friends share our spiritual goals and values.

If you are married, here's another suggestion: make your spouse your best friend. As a married person, it is certainly okay to have other friends, but your spouse needs to be your best friend. That does not mean you do everything with your spouse, but it does mean that the most meaningful things you would get from a friendship—the strongest examples of empathy, caring, love, understanding, admonitions to be the best you can be, and special times together—come from your spouse.

Also, if you're married you should take care with friendships with the opposite sex. Don't have a best friend of the opposite sex (other than your mate). The marriage bond is too important, the intimacy built up over the years too fragile to risk. If there are needs you are having fulfilled by a member of the opposite sex who is not your spouse, then it's best you turn to your spouse to have those fulfilled. And if your spouse can't supply them, then strongly consider going without or meeting some of those needs with your same-sex friends..

Of course, there's nothing wrong with having friends of the opposite sex, those you speak to occasionally at gatherings on "couples dates," or at work, who care about how you're doing and whom you care about. But be careful about going anywhere one-on-one with a member of the opposite sex. You should not stop after work for a cup of coffee with them, go on business trips alone with them, speak on the phone with them except for relatively brief periods of time, or put yourself in any way at risk with them. Guarding your marriage is one of the single most important things you do, and rules like these will help tremendously in the long run. Your best friends, other than your mate, should be same-sex friends.

## DO SOMETHING NICE FREQUENTLY

Doing something nice for others is part of building relationships, but it's also just a neat way to live your life. And, as you can imagine, frequently doing something nice should start with your spouse and children. Now and again do one of your spouse's chores—make the bed, or empty the dishwasher, or clean the office area, whatever. And don't make a big deal out of it; just let them find it done. Maybe buy your kids a little gift they've wanted, or do one of their chores, or take them someplace they've wanted to go.

Then do something for other members of your family, then for your friends.

Little things. Things they would enjoy but won't make them feel guilty that they have put you out. Maybe your brother likes motorcycles, so you buy him a motorcycle magazine or tickets to a cycle show. Or maybe your parents need their garage or the gutters cleaned—so you spend a Saturday morning doing that.

Random acts of kindness are fun too. Pay the toll for the guy in back of you, or give a good parking space to the lady behind you while you find another one. The list of possibilities is endless. Of course, even more fun than the random acts are the premeditated acts of kindness: the birthday party for the new person at work, cutting the neighbor's lawn, taking an elderly person to a movie. These are acts of kindness that you know will be appreciated and will bring you closer to people.

You may also enjoy doing secret acts of kindness, where the person you do something nice for never knows it was you who did it. Only God and you will know. Some say these acts of kindness return the best feelings of all.

And there is as much benefit for you as there is for the person you're helping. You feel better, your brain amines get a shot in the arm, and the world, particularly the part of it that you inhabit, is just a happier place.

## GUIDELINE 4
## DEAL WITH ANGER

In the last chapter, we looked at where anger comes from and how to determine when it is appropriate. Here we want to give you four steps that will help you deal properly with your anger.

### 1. ADMIT YOU'RE ANGRY.

You would be surprised how many people come in for counseling who have all the earmarks of being angry but just won't admit it. "I'm not angry, just frustrated." Or, "I'm a Christian. I'm not supposed to be angry." Well, Christians do get angry. And they get angry at people they shouldn't.

Anger is a natural reaction to many, many situations. It may be an inappropriate reaction sometimes, but it is a common reaction. So, the first thing you do is admit your anger. There's no need to hide it. God knows it's there. Admitting it to yourself does no harm, and it's the first step in doing yourself a lot of good.

### 2. DECIDE IF YOUR ANGER IS APPROPRIATE.

Identify and categorize your anger. Is it due to perfectionism, selfishness, paranoia, or due to righteous indignation? As you do this, by the process of elimination you will decide if your anger is justified—or which part of your anger is. (It can sometimes be a combination of all of the above categories).

### 3. IF YOU HAVE BEHAVED INAPPROPRIATELY BECAUSE OF YOUR ANGER, MAKE IMMEDIATE AMENDS.

Even if your anger is justified, you may have allowed it to take control. You may have exploded in someone's face, or thrown things, or threatened someone, or done any one of a hundred other things of which you are now ashamed. If that's true—and particularly if your anger is not justified—make amends with the person you have wronged immediately. Go to him or her, or them, with your hat in hand and apologize for your outburst. "I was angry. I lost control and I'm terribly sorry. What I did was not appropriate for a Christian, and I deeply regret it."

## 4. IF YOUR ANGER IS APPROPRIATE, DO THE GODLY THING.

If you have been wronged, the first place to start is with forgiveness. Go to the Lord and sincerely ask Him to work in your heart and mind to restore your sense of love for the person who has wronged you. That may not be easy. If you have been wronged in a terrible and personal way, forgiveness might be a difficult, rocky road. Remember, forgiveness does not mean you are condoning what that person has done. It just means you are turning vengeance over to God and giving up your personal right to retaliate. You are wiping the slate clean and trusting God to take care of it.

Next, determine what your ongoing relationship with the person should be. If it's someone close to you, like your spouse, then it's very appropriate that you discuss the infraction with him or her and deal with it in a loving, but firm way. If your spouse is wronging you, hopefully your spouse will be sincerely interested in changing (but don't count on it).

If your anger is a result of someone else having been wronged, then you need to offer your help to that person in the same way Jesus would. You bring comfort, love, and the gospel of Jesus Christ. But also, if at all possible, you minister to the perpetrator, the one doing the wrong. Since he may be the one with the hardest heart, bring him in prayer before the Lord— pray that his heart might be pierced for Jesus. If you have the opportunity to minister to the wrongdoer, make sure you bring the Lord with you—and bring Him with thanksgiving for using you in this way.

Another responsibility you might have, and you have to decide if this effort is appropriate, is to help change the system that allowed the wrong to be done in the first place. As Christians, our job is not necessarily to change the social structures; our job is to spread the gospel within the world system. But sometimes by helping those who are being exploited, you earn the right to be heard. By feeding the hungry, you earn the right to feed their souls.

One of the key elements of leading a happy, balanced life is dealing with the anger that crops up, and we have gone through the ways you can constructively do that. However, the best way to deal with anger is to lead a life that minimizes it. And the best way to do that is to foster a close, loving relationship with your Lord. The closer you are to the Lord, the closer your life and attitudes mirror those of Jesus. The anger of Jesus was, and still is, always appropriate, always generated with just the right amount of heat, and always directed to the right person or persons. Our goal as Christians is to do the same.

## GUIDELINE 5
## TURN TOWARD GOD DAILY

The previous four guidelines showed how to live our lives as part of a social structure. They suggested ways to make our lives more balanced, how to build our support groups among family and friends, then went on to suggest how to deal with anger toward those who offend us. These first four guidelines had us looking inward. This final one asks us to look up—toward God. And since God and your relationship with Him are the two most important things in your life, it stands to reason that this guideline is the most important.

We can sum up guideline number five by saying, "In everything you do, glorify Christ." The apostle Paul put it this way: "So whether you eat or drink or whatever you do, do it all for the glory of God" (1 Cor. 10:31 NIV).

It's so easy to say, and it sounds so good, but what does it really mean to do everything for the glory of God? Let's find out by seeing how Brenda, and later Melinda, made this guideline a pivotal part of their lives.

As she began to implement the guidelines in her own life, Brenda took this one very seriously. Realizing that her low-level depression, which led to her irritability and impatience, would be best counteracted by a complete and total commitment to Jesus, she decided to put much of her efforts here.

So she carefully mapped out what she would do to glorify Christ in all she did. Here is her plan.

Every morning Brenda faithfully takes twenty minutes to have her devotional. Then she prays. It's generally a wide-ranging prayer that depends, like all our prayers, on what is on her mind that particular morning. But her prayer also contains some specifics. First is a commitment to serve Jesus in every way she can during the day. She also prays that God the Father will help her become more like Jesus that day. She prays for God to help her avoid hurting anyone that day, and to avoid sin. She also prays that when frustrating things happen, because they do happen most days, God will help her learn from them rather than stuffing her anger and getting depressed.

Before, when she rose from bed, the day lay before her like a dragon she would have to slay. Everything she was called upon to do was a chore. Even when Brenda was between her moods, every aspect of the day was something to be conquered, something to be endured, something placed there by an indifferent God to be more of a gauntlet than a blessing.

But now all that has changed. Brenda sees each day as a gift, presented to her by a loving God eager to see her serve and grow closer to Him. Rather than a dragon with hot, fiery breath, the day is a wonderful garden to be nurtured and enjoyed. Granted, it's a viewpoint that might have caused Pollyanna to be called a pessimist, but when you view the day like that, when you see that all things really do work to the good of those who love God and are called according to His purpose, then the day takes on a whole new look. It really can be seen as a wonder stretching before you.

Now, does that mean Brenda's day is all sunshine and flowers? No. There's the same spilled milk, the same scattered books, even now and again the same current of depression, but now they take on a different meaning. Before, these things were evidence of that dragon breathing fire at her and standing between her and what she wanted to get done. Now they're happening for a reason. They are evidence that the Lord is teaching her patience—a loving Father working with her to make her a better person. That does not mean the old reflexes are not at work, but because she is naturally more relaxed about things—even during those rare times now when the irritability returns—she is far less likely to lose control and far more likely to shrug those difficult times off, particularly in the morning.

At a recent women's ministry meeting, Brenda gave her testimony. "Our job," she told the ladies gathered there, "is to take everything that comes and turn it into praise for the Lord and a furthering of His gospel." She went on to tell them the story of how she came unglued when Hannah's car door wouldn't open. "I thought my witness was destroyed that day— I was such an idiot screaming and banging on the door. Well, a couple of weeks ago it was raining and I drove Hannah to school. She got out and I was about to pull away when I saw a woman doing just as I had done. She was obviously at the end of her rope and was standing out by her car, the rain pelting down, trying desperately to get the door open for her child. Like I had done, she was screaming at the lock, banging on the window.

"Had it not happened to me, I might have laughed. But I knew just what she was going through. I grabbed my umbrella and got out of the car, then splashed my way over to her and held the umbrella for her. After a few words, she began to calm down. We have become friends and I've been sharing the Lord with her. She's not all that receptive, but these things take time.

"I guess what I'm trying to say is that if you believe everything happens to us for a reason, you'll begin to see the Lord's reason in everything. Even when we do dumb things, even sinful things, God will find ways to glorify Himself through them. Our job, then, is just to work with Him and take Him up on the opportunities that present themselves."

## GETTING INVOLVED IN MINISTRY

Even though Melinda and Don did a lot of talking and even more reconciling, there was a residue of hurt that lingered for Melinda. She found it hard to completely forgive Don for deliberately hurting her. Although she knew God wanted her to forgive, and she also knew that Don had repented and was doing the best he could to make it up to her, there were still times when the depression returned. Certainly not to the depths as before, but still at levels that caused her to take a walk through a very shadowy valley now and again.

When she made this guideline a part of her life, Melinda wanted to use it as a way to submerge herself in God's love and to take her mind away from those places where depression lurked, hoping to snare her again.

She, too, began turning toward God daily through prayer and the Word, but she also decided to bring glory to the Lord through action. She called her pastor and got involved in ministry at the church. Melinda enjoyed crafts, so she began teaching a crafts class during lunchtime. The class became so popular that she began teaching another one in the evening as well. Since the classes were held at the church, it introduced the church to those who came, and Melinda's faith, over time, introduced the students to Jesus, if they had not been believers already.

Since she was still plagued by an occasional bout of mild depression, she decided to involve herself in a support group. Through her pastor, Melinda found four other ladies who met once a week and discussed how the Lord was working in their lives. They would then support each other through any difficult times they might be facing. Melinda welcomed not only the support, but the accountability as well. When she found unforgiveness feeding her depression, the other ladies would help her deal with why forgiveness was so difficult. Over time, inch by inch, element by element, Melinda got to the place where she felt her old love for Don returning—the old warmth and intimacy becoming a part of their relationship again.

She did something else too. A friend of one of the ladies in her support group had an eighteen-year-old daughter—a girl who had recently gotten pregnant and married, in that order. Although both she and her husband loved the Lord, they were very young and needed the wisdom and guidance of someone Melinda's age and experience. Melinda offered to mentor the young lady. And she offered this not so much because she considered herself so wise, but because there is an added responsibility to keep your life on track when someone is looking to you for advice and counsel. Melinda wanted that added edge against slipping back to her old, depression-prone ways.

The last thing Melinda did, about a year after all these other things, was to take a leadership position with the women's ministry at church. Again, with many women now looking to her for godly leadership, it was that much more of a reason to keep her life in order.

As she was doing these things, she was sensing God's presence in her life growing more profound and meaningful. The more she did for Him, the more she glorified Him in her life, the more she walked by faith instead of by sight, and the more of Himself He revealed to her.

At the end of two years, Melinda was as far from a bout of depression as the east is from the west.

So, what does this mean for you?

The closer and more all-encompassing your walk with the Lord, the less likely you are to suffer from environmental moods and mood swings. Why? Because the closer you are to God, the more He is conforming you to the image of His Son.

Although the way you make this guideline a part of your life is an extremely personal thing—after all, the plan God has for your life is a very personal plan—there are certain steps Brenda and Melinda took that you can apply to your life. Here's a recap.

1. Begin the day with a commitment to Jesus and a commitment to become more like Him.

2. View the day—and even the trials of that day—as a gift from a loving God.

3. Look for and take opportunities to glorify Jesus around you.

4. Realize you are going to slip sometimes, so become part of an accountability support group.

5. Become active in a ministry to others, using whatever talent God has gifted you with.

6. Mentor someone.

7. Allow the Lord to work, realizing it might take some time and might occur at a slow, inch-by-inch pace, but always keep in mind how far you've come.

## STUDY THE WORD OF GOD DAILY

We have saved this item for last, but it is actually one of the most important things anyone can do for good mental health, and that is to meditate on God's Word daily. The Bible is God's love letter to us, and it is powerful, showing us our innermost thoughts and unconscious motives.

Meditating on Scripture every day is a habit that will serve you well for the rest of your life.

Let's turn now to some spiritual principles that will help you reach wholeness and wellness—and stay there.

# 14 SEVEN KEYS TO SPIRITUAL RENEWAL

There is no greater threat to someone who suffers from either environmentally caused or genetically caused moods and mood swings than stress. When stress mounts within us, all our negative instincts take over and war against all the work we've ever done to lead more balanced and godly lives. Much of what we have set out to accomplish in this book is to help you define a life for yourself that is as stress-free as possible. And our hope is that you have implemented those suggestions and are well on your way to leading such a life.

But there is one more thing to do to safeguard yourself—to bring yourself into a fortress that will never fail you. We would like to introduce you to that fortress and give you its keys— seven keys to be exact.

## KEY 1
### SURRENDER

Allowing God to Help Me Grow As I Submit to His Authority

*Therefore humble yourselves under the mighty hand of God,*
*that He may exalt you in due time.*
1 Peter 5:6 NKJV

God is the Creator of life and the Lord of the universe. But ever since the Garden of Eden, men and women have continually played God and have tried, unsuccessfully, to rule over their own destinies. From Genesis through Revelation, Scripture reveals humankind's natural incapacity to live healthy, God-pleasing lives. The Old Testament describes a colorful assortment of characters who turned their backs on God's ways and inevitably experienced fear, foolishness, and failure. Fortunately, some of them surrendered to the ultimate power of God, allowing Him to intervene in their lives with divine power and wisdom. In the New Testament, Christ's death on the cross made God's intervention even more accessible: He took upon Himself the willfulness and rebellion of the entire world. His resurrection brought hope for a new life.

When we eventually realize that the road we have chosen is not taking us where we need to go, we also understand that to stay on this road is to choose further heartache and destruction. At this point, we are willing to admit that our lives have spun out of control, that self-control has failed us, and that our forms of self-treatment have failed us and must be abandoned. Fortunately, while we are limited, God is not. By acknowledging that He alone has the power to change the course of our lives, and that we are powerless to change it ourselves, we surrender to Him and begin the process of spiritual renewal.

The first key to spiritual renewal and transformation is thus surrender.

Surrender means:

- humbling ourselves before the God of the universe

- admitting that God is all-powerful, and releasing our struggles to Him

- refusing to escape into the old patterns, habits, and attitudes that continue to push us toward destructive directions in our lives

- no longer saying, "I can handle this myself"

- submitting to God's way of doing things, even though we don't understand it

- getting past our pain and fear and clinging to hope in God and His love for us

- setting aside our human understanding and becoming childlike, acknowledging that we have no answers that work

Evidence of a lack of surrender includes:

- guilt over the past

- fear of the future

- anger over others

Only when we surrender our lives to God can we fully accept the reality of our own lives. And that is the second key to spiritual renewal.

## KEY 2
### ACCEPTANCE

Accepting the Full Reality of My Situation

> *O LORD, You have searched me and known me.*
> Psalm 139:1 NKJV

As we begin to acknowledge the grim futility of our existence and the abandonment of God's ways that led to it, our eyes begin to open. We see that our lives are dangerously at risk. Through self-examination we confront our sins, character defects, habits, and areas of irresponsibility, becoming aware that if we had not changed our course, we would be headed toward physical, emotional, and spiritual disaster.

All of us struggle with blind spots in our lives, and to some degree we all live in denial and self-deception. Rather than seeing our areas of sin and pain, we tend to point to others and focus on them, or we find ways to distract or anesthetize ourselves. God wants us to look at the "big lie" of our lives, realizing that the road we're on is actually a detour we have taken to avoid facing our own hurts and failures. That detour can involve many things that keep us from growing spiritually. Breaking through denial means becoming aware of our sin and our pain, and consciously confronting the sick behaviors and patterns that have detoured us.

Once, with God's help, we remove our blinders, deception and denial come to an end, and we begin to see ourselves as we really are: trapped in our sins, paralyzed by fear, and doing things that produce short-term results rather than long-term change. We also come to see God as He is: patient, longing, and "able to do exceedingly abundantly above all that we ask or think" (Eph. 3:20 NKJV).

By facing ourselves honestly, we move out of the past and into the reality of the present, where God will teach us to resolve our problems rather than reproduce them in family and close friends.

Seeing the reality of my situation helps me to focus on what I can do to change rather than on what I want others to do to make me feel better. It means becoming humble enough to confront who I really am, what my motives really are, and what really causes the conflicts I experience. Thus the second key to spiritual renewal and transformation is acceptance.

Acceptance means:

- not lying to ourselves about the failures, sins, and heartaches in our lives, and acknowledging the truth about our situation

- considering what we criticize in others as a clue to what we may be denying in ourselves

- facing our past, our pain, and our failures head-on

- not blaming others for our difficulties

- seeking, receiving, and applying God's wisdom

- looking at what we have done in the light of God's mercy and grace

- accepting that we are unable to help ourselves without God's help

- naming our character defects and mistakes rather than denying them

Evidence of a lack of acceptance includes:

- constant criticism of others

- confusion over why people react to you and what you say

- repeated lying

Acceptance allows us to be open and transparent and leads us to healing.

## KEY 3
## CONFESSION

Beginning to Open Up About the Reality of My Life

*Confess your trespasses to one another, and pray for one another, that you may be healed.*
James 5:16 NKJV

There is sickness in secrecy. The sinning psalmist, King David, said, "When I kept silent, my bones wasted away through my groaning all day long" (Psalm 32:3 NIV). By breaking our silence and speaking the truth about ourselves aloud to another person, we move out of the darkness and bring our secrets into the light. Confessing our sins and talking about the sins done to us by others is one key to spiritual healing and emotional health.

It is clearly important to God that men and women verbally express the struggles hidden in their hearts. Verbalization gives substance to inarticulate thoughts, and words affirm the realities of which we have become aware. Even on the key issue of Christian salvation, belief is to be affirmed with spoken words. Paul wrote, "If you confess with your mouth, 'Jesus is Lord,' and believe in your heart that God raised him from the dead, you will be saved. For it is with your heart that you believe and are justified, and it is with your mouth that you confess and are saved" (Romans 10: 9–10 NIV).

In similar terms, when we confess our sins, the words we speak give a concrete dimension to subtle compromises and behaviors that might otherwise remain unclear in our minds. By telling others of sins and shortcoming in our lives, we confirm our awareness of those faults, and we become obedient to God's ways of working in the lives of His children. Unexpressed thoughts are exempt from the input of other Christians who can both challenge and help us to see the truth. When we confess our faults, we put others in the position of advising us, praying for us, and sharing our struggles.

Confession requires openness, and openness requires vulnerability. Confession also requires confidentiality. Confession is an invitation to intimacy, and it involves trust in both God and another person—a trust that is necessary for us to fully reveal our secrets. Unless we open ourselves, whatever help we receive from others will not thoroughly address our real needs and conflicts. Openness is an outward act of trust that enables us to cleanse our sores from the inside out. The third key to spiritual renewal and transformation is confession.

Confession means:

- submitting ourselves to God's way of handling secrets, respecting His desire for openness and vulnerability among His people

- being willing to overcome our fear of rejection by revealing our failures to another person

- admitting to at least one other person that we have fallen short of God's best, including our character defects and judgment errors

- not trying to mask our true feelings

- choosing to humble ourselves before both God and others

- renouncing our independence and admitting that we need help from fellow believers

- putting our vague sense of guilt into written or spoken words and expressing the situation without making excuses

Evidence of a lack of confession includes:

- lack of connectedness with others

- superficial interactions with others

- fear of being found out

When we have confessed, then we can take responsibility for our lives.

## KEY 4
## RESPONSIBILITY

Taking Responsibility to Make Necessary Changes for Spiritual Growth to Occur

*For each one shall bear his own load.*
Galatians 6:5 NKJV

Taking responsibility for our problems entails two realities: experience and ownership. In many instances, the hurts that have driven us into inappropriate behaviors and destructive habits are hurts we have never fully worked through. We have spent our lives diverting ourselves from problems and anesthetizing our emotions with harmful substances, hurtful people, and activities. Although it requires God-given courage to walk through our pain and to grieve our losses, the process of doing so is an indispensable element in our healing.

We live in a world where people take on the role of victim and live out a life of victimization. Yet as horrendous as our past problems and abuses may have been, when we own them as part of ourselves, we learn to see them as purposeful, deepening, and integral to our development of godly character. As the psalmist wrote, "It is good for me that I have been afflicted, / That I may learn Your statutes" (Psalm 119:71 NKJV).

Avoidance of pain and problems is a natural human response. Most people feel they have "suffered enough" and have no desire to feel overwhelmed by sorrowful emotions. But grief is a necessary process in a fallen world, and grief over our failures and losses will connect us to God's grace. No one experienced more grief and pain than Jesus as He agonized in the garden and shed His blood on the cross. St. Augustine affirmed this, saying, "In my deepest wound I saw Your glory, and it dazzled me."

How easy it is to point to our past pain as an excuse to miss God's plan. It is also easy to blame others around us for everything that has gone wrong. Accepting responsibility is a bold step where we take the reality of our lives and allow God to use it to change us. He shapes us into His character as we follow His ways. The fourth key to spiritual renewal and transformation is responsibility.

Taking responsibility means:

- facing our problems rather than escaping them

- taking the time to grieve our losses and experience pain

- believing Jesus' words: "Blessed are those who mourn, / For they shall be comforted" (Matt. 5:4 NKJV)

- not playing the role of victim

- being willing to bear the full responsibility of our misconduct

- not blaming others for our sins

- reaching out to Jesus, who is fully capable of understanding our emotional pain, having suffered abuse and rejection Himself

- looking beyond our losses at God's deeper purposes

- accepting the hope that God's plans for us are always good and loving

- refusing to allow anything from our past to be an excuse for lack of growth or character development

Evidence of a lack of responsibility includes:

- constantly finding yourself a victim of others' actions

- blaming others for ongoing difficulties

- involvement with destructive substances, people, and activities in a futile attempt to deaden pain

Taking responsibility also means that we forgive ourselves as well as others.

## KEY 5

### FORGIVENESS

Forgiving My Own Failures and the Failures of Those Who Have Hurt Me

> For if you forgive men their trespasses,
> your heavenly Father will also forgive you.
> Matthew 6:14 NKJV

To forgive and to receive forgiveness are gracious acts of love. These acts have supernatural power to change both the life of the forgiven and the one who forgives. When we look at how God has forgiven us, it moves us to find a way to forgive others, even if they have hurt us deeply. The cross of Jesus allows this in a dimension far beyond our own power to forgive.

Forgiveness is inextricably interwoven into Christian salvation. Jesus clearly taught that unless we forgive others, we cannot be forgiven by our Heavenly Father. At first glance, this may appear to be a rigid and rigorous principle, but it is God's means of extending His grace to everyone. When we refuse to forgive, we play "god" in the lives of others and pass judgment on them. This interferes with the process of grace Jesus initiated at the cross.

Forgiveness can be difficult—almost impossible—for those who have been severely abused physically, sexually, and even spiritually. It is never easy or instant, and it may take years to complete. However, if forgiveness is not rendered, the injured person remains trapped in the abuse of the past. Additionally, choosing not to forgive allows others to continue to abuse us, as we endlessly relive their offenses. Our yesterdays must be put in the past so we can fully enjoy today.

The forgiveness process also involves making things right with those we have wounded. This may require us to write letters or make phone calls, to repay debts, to make amends, or otherwise do our part in making wrongs as right as possible. This, of course, can result in enormous spiritual blessings, both to others and to us.

Forgiveness, when empowered by God's Spirit, is a process of detaching painful events from our emotional response to them, thus facilitating the process of healing. In contrast, the refusal to forgive has far-reaching results spiritually, emotionally, and even physically. Lack of forgiveness (bitterness, grudges, vengeful motives, repressed anger) is the primary cause of most depressions. The fifth key to spiritual renewal and transformation is forgiveness.

Forgiveness means:

- handing back our rights to God (the rights we usurped from Him) and inviting Him to be in charge

- asking for forgiveness and making restitution for the damage we have done

- not energizing ourselves with rage or hatred

- not trying to change other people but asking God to do it if He wants to and if they cooperate with God

- stepping out of the past and into the present

- accepting the pardon of the Cross for others as well as for ourselves

- obeying Jesus' instructions to forgive so that we can be forgiven

- beginning a process of forgiveness which may continue for a lifetime

- living in the light of God's forgiveness

- sifting through our lives and discarding the resentments and hurts of the past

Evidence of a lack of forgiveness includes:

- continuing to hold a grudge against others

- failing to make restitution for past wrongs

- feeling that God is angry at you personally

Forgiveness may be difficult, but it leads us to complete transformation.

## KEY 6
### TRANSFORMATION

Transforming My Pain into a Purposeful Mission out of My Desire to Share with Others and Love Them

> *Blessed be the God and Father of our Lord Jesus Christ,*
> *the Father of mercies and God of all comfort, who*
> *comforts us in all our tribulation, that we may be able to*
> *comfort those who are in any trouble, with the comfort with*
> *which we ourselves are comforted by God.*
> 2 Corinthians 1:3–4 NKJV

SEVEN KEYS TO SPIRITUAL RENEWAL

We can never know God's plans, or His gain from our loss, unless we give Him our misery and allow Him to transform it into a mission for our lives. Once our loss and pain point us to God's grace, we can also lead others into His grace. In doing so, we partner with God as He accomplishes His purpose. After we emerge from our own despair, become transparent, and candidly share our victories, we will be in a position to share our struggles and God's power to overcome, attracting others into His grace.

The gospel of Christ brings a profound message about earthly evil beings transformed into eternal good: weakness into strength, tragedy into triumph, loss into gain, mortality into immortality, death into life. These concepts might be superficially discounted as theological abstractions, except that they translate into inescapable day-by-day "miracles" that are clearly evident in the lives of Christian believers throughout the world.

The cosmic turning point in the transformation of evil-to-good is the death and resurrection of Jesus. We activate this process in our personal lives through faith in God's Son, through hope in His good and loving character, and through relinquishment of our lives to His flawless will.

Once we have surrendered ourselves to the power and love of God, we become aware of the profound changes and new avenues of hope He has created in our lives. Once we have forgiven others, our most difficult experiences leave us with a greater capacity for empathy and compassion. Our ability to love has deepened. We have become more honest. Now our hearts are full of gratitude. Living in the grace God has given us, becoming aware of the gifts of the Spirit, and feeling the joy of spiritual renewal, we are compelled to carry the wonderful message of spiritual transformation to others. We reverse and defuse our own heartaches and losses by reaching out to those facing struggles similar to our own. Unless we give away our miracle to others, we stifle God's message and miss out on God's blessings for us. The sixth key to spiritual renewal is thus transformation.

Transformation means:

- stepping out of our own pain and into the needs of others

- participating in God's process of working all things together for good

- seeking ways of applying past pain to positive purposes

- not saying "Why me, Lord?" but saying, "What do you want me to do, Lord?"

- being a giver instead of a taker

- learning to listen rather than always needing to be heard

- allowing our humbling experiences to give us a servant's heart

- investing our spiritual gifts in the lives of others

- discovering our God-given spiritual gifts and using those gifts in reaching and serving others

Evidence of a lack of transformation includes:

- living without meaning or purpose; feeling life is a waste

- being unaware of spiritual gifts and talents or how to use them

- remaining self-obsessed and without loving feelings for others

## KEY 7
## PRESERVATION

Protecting the Spiritual Gains I Have Made and Persevering Through Life's Inevitable Struggles

*For this very reason, make every effort to add to your faith goodness; and to goodness, knowledge; and to knowledge, self-control; and to self-control, perseverance; and to perseverance, godliness; and to godliness, brotherly kindness; and to brotherly kindness, love. For if you possess these qualities in increasing measure, they will keep you from being ineffective and unproductive in your knowledge of our Lord Jesus Christ.*
2 Peter 1:5–8 NIV

The process of surrendering to God's love and authority is a lifelong process. By the time we have made our way through the process of spiritual transformation, we know that we need other Christians to help us stay on the right path. Without them, we are likely to return to patterns of secrecy, sin, and sickness. When we place ourselves in a position of accountability to others, we invite their scrutiny. At first this goes against our natural bent and seems like an invasion of our privacy. But accountability to others is an invaluable means of preventing a recurrence of our sinful behavior. The removal of "secrets" from our lives was essential to our healing. Now we need to introduce spiritual disciplines into our lives so that we are not entrapped by either overconfidence or a return to secret sins.

Paul wrote, "Be decent and true in everything you do so that all can approve of your behavior . . . ask the Lord Jesus Christ to help you live as you should, and don't make plans to enjoy evil. (Rom. 13:13–14 TLB)." We are able to remain "decent and true" only because God is with us, upholding us and giving us new life. By continually surrendering to His will, and through ongoing and honest accountability to trustworthy individuals, we are able to take the message of renewal and transformation to other hurting people, never forgetting where we came from and how we got where we are.

Scripture indicates that human willfulness is at odds with God's plan for His people. He created us to be entirely dependent upon Him, continuing to repent from our sins, and to return to His ways. He wants us to communicate with Him in prayer. He has also indicated in His description of the multidimensional body of Christ (1 Cor. 12, Rom. 12), that we are meant to be dependent upon other Christians. Our sinful human nature has always given us the message that we can handle life quite well on our own. However, God's Word and painful experiences remind us that we cannot. The seventh key to spiritual renewal and transformation is preservation.

Preservation means:

- establishing boundaries that prevent our return to sick and sinful behaviors

- continuing to forgive and to be forgiven

- avoiding secrecy by remaining accountable to others, while being a trustworthy confidant for their secrets

- choosing to be part of a godly community

- reading God's Word, meditating upon it, praying daily, and practicing spiritual discipline

- developing, with God's help, a deep and godly character

- being patient with ourselves when we slip

- moving forward while remembering where we've been

- continuing the process of surrender—day by day, year by year

Evidence of a lack of preservation includes:

- no accountable relationships

- no established boundaries to eliminate risky situations

- lack of involvement in spiritual disciplines

We have all heard the phrase, "This is the first day of the rest of your life." As we write this, it sounds trite, yet at no time in your history has this been any more true for you than it is right now. If you have been plagued by moods and mood swings in the past, now you're looking forward to a life of freedom. In some cases there might be some medications you will have to take. Perhaps you will have to watch what is happening to you more closely than you have before, but these are minor inconveniences when compared to the prison of emotions you used to call home. Today a life of service to yourself, your family, and your God is laid out before you. Our prayers go with you.

If, on the other hand, you decided to read to this point before deciding to take the journey we have mapped out, the time has come for commitment. We urge you to make it. We urge you to begin again at Chapter One and work your way back to this point. And when you get here a second time, our prayer is that you have left your moods and mood swings back along the way somewhere, and your life of emotional freedom is stretching out ahead of you.

In either case, the future belongs to you and will be far more fulfilling because you have decided with God's help to master your moods.

# PART 4

# LIVING
# VICTORIOUSLY
## WITH A BIPOLAR
## SPECTRUM DISORDER

# 15 FINDING THE HELP YOU NEED

These remaining chapters are written especially for those who suffer from one of the bipolar spectrum disorders and for their families. If you suffer from genetically caused moods and mood swings, we want to congratulate you for coming with us on this journey to wellness.

And if you have been plowing your way through the exercises in this book, you have already done a lot of work. You have attacked any environmentally caused depression and irritability you might have been experiencing, and you have given yourself tools to combat them whenever they reoccur. And they will. All of us, no matter how "together" we might like to think we are, now and again get at least somewhat depressed, irritable, and restless.

In the last section you learned how to build a foundation upon which to lay the tracks for the rest of your trip—working your way through your bipolar spectrum disorder to complete wellness.

Complete wellness is not just a pipe dream. It is very possible that within the next few weeks or months you will be managing your emotions instead of dreading your moods. Our experience shows that success depends on two things. First, you must avail yourself of good, insight-oriented therapy—the kind that digs for issues of anger and shame and emphasizes forgiveness and setting reasonable boundaries to prevent future abuses. Second, after you connect with quality, loving people, you should take the proper medication. By doing these two things, many of bipolar sufferers will recover without additional treatment other than lifelong medication management. If engaged in daily therapy sessions, recovery could be in a few weeks. Others will start improving in a week or two but require about a year to reach "happiness peak." In all, it takes about fifty hours of therapy on average to reach that goal.

Now that's exciting.

So, this chapter is meant to help you make those first essential steps. They include:

- guidelines for choosing a good psychiatrist or counselor

- a general discussion on medications

- an encouragement for discipline

Choosing a competent professional to work with you through this all-important stage of your journey is a critical task. Of course, you should feel free to call one of our clinics; the numbers are listed in the back of this book. Or you could ask your friends if they have had experience with a good counselor, or ask your pastor. Psychiatrists and counselors know that good rapport between counselor and patient is important, so they will not mind if you ask lots of questions during your first evaluation session. They will probably have quite a few for you as well.

Ideally, your therapist should be a well-rounded person, one who has had experience with life, one who is not too directive or too passive. One who gives you ample opportunity to speak, and one who gently guides rather than prods—unless, of course, prodding is needed. One who is honest about his or her own feelings and open, vulnerable, spiritual, and reflective. One who is not prone to jump to conclusions and pigeonhole you, but rather is able to look at you as a unique person.

We suggest you ask the psychiatrist and therapist what other experience they have had with bipolar clients and if they are up on the new medications. For example, some psychiatrists who are not up on the newer meds tend to put all their bipolar patients on lithium, even though it does not work on rapid cyclers, only works on fifty percent of bipolars, and has lots of potentially dangerous side effects. Lithium is still the best medication for some, but there are newer and safer bipolar meds (like Depakote and Neurontin, for example).

When you make your decision, you need to work closely and honestly with your counselor (for therapy) and with your psychiatrist (for meds). If you want a counselor who digs, you need to dig with him—and trust us, some of that digging may be painful.

Also, don't delay in doing any of this. The longer your bipolar disorder persists unchecked, the more difficult it is to treat because the manic and depressive cycles become longer, more frequent, and more severe if left unmedicated.

## MEDICATIONS

Since we initially began defining the bipolar spectrum disorders with ADHD, the kissing cousin of bipolar, we will begin with it here as well.

### *ADHD*
Sometimes depressed individuals also have ADHD. These individuals may be helped by sustained-release bupropion

(Wellbutrin-SR) or sustained-release venlafaxine (Effexor-XR), both of which build up the norepinephrine level and, may help ADHD. Effexor-XR also builds up serotonin, which may help eliminate headaches, PMS, and anxiety. We have seen many of our ADHD high school and college-age patients go from C to A averages with taking these meds. One ADHD depressed patient recently flunked out of college because he could not concentrate or get organized. After a few weeks on Wellbutrin-SR (150 milligrams every morning), he went back to college and got all As. In general, this medication has very few side effects, which often disappear within a week or two, after the body adjusts to the dosage. (Wellbutrin-SR is not recommended for people with epilepsy because it can enhance the possibility of a seizure, but Effexor-XR can be given to most people with epilepsy.)

Effexor-XR is more difficult than most antidepressants to withdraw from if it is found to not work; it can cause flu-like symptoms for a few days if withdrawn too quickly. We suggest withdrawing it over a week or more in gradually decreasing doses. But if either of these meds works well, the adult ADHD patient can stay on it for life, since ADHD is most likely genetic and lifelong in most cases.

Let's turn now to the bipolar spectrum disorders and see what help there is for people like Brenda and Wendy.

## BIPOLAR SPECTRUM DISORDERS

Many bipolar patients should receive lifelong medications in order to experience the best possible quality of life. Most bipolar I patients should, and many bipolar II, cyclothymic, and genetic dysthymic patients should as well, not only to increase their quality of life but also to prevent, or at least decrease, the likelihood that the condition will grow worse over the years.

## MEDICATION FOR THE HIGHS

Although lithium and Depakote are often prescribed and are considered equally effective in the treatment of manic or mixed episodes (a manic episode with irritable or unhappy moods), we suggest Depakote as a first choice for all types of bipolar illness unless it just won't work. We often recommend it because it has fewer side effects overall and is not as difficult as lithium to administer and maintain, which makes compliance by the patient much easier.

Usually either Depakote or lithium will help significantly within a few weeks. If neither one works separately, your doctor may either switch to the other one, or combine both, or combine one of them with Tegretol (carbamazepine). If Depakote did not work for some reason, we might consider using one of the newer bipolar medications, such as Neurontin (gabapentin), which is very often safe and effective. Neurontin often has been used as an augmentation agent in bipolar disorders.

## INSOMNIA

For insomnia and agitation during a manic episode, your doctor will probably use either antianxiety medicines, such as Klonopin (clonazepam) or Ativan (lorazepam), or antipsychotic medications, such as Zyprexa, Seroquel or Risperdal (risperidone).

We sometimes suggest Klonopin first, because it is less addicting than Ativan, often has no other side effects, and generally is safer than the major tranquilizers. We also may suggest Ambien for sleep, along with some Klonopin, since Ambien is not normally as addictive as some of the other major tranquilizers. Benzodiazepine sleeping pills (like ProSom) are another option. We often do not use the old antipsychotic meds because of potential side effects. The atypical antipsychotic agents (Zyrexa, Seroquel, or Risperdal) prove safer for many patients.

## DELUSIONS, HALLUCINATIONS, OR SEVERE AGITATION

However, if you have delusions, hallucinations, or severe agitation, we suggest your doctor add an antipsychotic or atypical antipsychotic medication to the mood stabilizer until these severe symptoms are totally gone. These powerful medications can help very quickly, sometimes within hours, making the two or three weeks we typically wait for the mood stabilizers to fully take effect seem like an eternity. We prefer the newer atypical antipsychotic medications (such as Seroquel, Risperdal, or Zyprexa) because they are overall safer than the old antipsychotic meds (such as Haldol, Navane, Mellaril, or Trilafon). Neurontin may also prove to be helpful, especially in combination with an atypical antipsychotic agent.

## PREAUTHORIZATION FOR MEDICATION

Some patients have to receive medication by injection, and against their will, because they do not understand how dangerous they are to themselves and others. Because recent court decisions have allowed some types of psychotic people to remain mentally ill even though they are not competent to make a decision, the doctor may be walking a fine line between restoring the sufferer's health and allowing him or her to remain psychotic until he kills himself, someone else, or becomes a homeless person. If you experience such episodes, it may be best to preauthorize treatment for yourself and have written preauthorization with your doctor or with responsible members of your family.

## ANTIANXIETY AND ANTIPSYCHOTIC MEDICATIONS

Antianxiety, antipsychotic, and atypical antipsychotic medications can cause drowsiness, but this is usually a blessing during an acute episode as it helps to calm the sufferer. But drowsiness is not a good thing after recovery. Remaining disciplined and taking your medication is difficult enough without having to deal with being sleepy all the time. Usually the sedation wears off after taking one of these meds for a week or so.

Antipsychotic medications can have a variety of other side effects:

- involuntary tongue or other muscle movement

- muscle stiffness

- restlessness

But normally you don't have to live with these. Your doctor can usually adjust the dosage, add a side-effect-blocking medication like Cogentin, or switch to a different medication.

As the patient recovers, the mood stabilizers become more prominent within ten days to three weeks, and the antidepressant medications may eliminate many of the depressive symptoms within one to four weeks. Antidepressants usually take about one to three months to reach maximum benefit, so we encourage our patients to be patient while they are waiting several weeks for the depression to disappear.

The benzodiazepine (antianxiety) meds and the antipsychotic or atypical antipsychotic meds, all of which generally work almost immediately, are sometimes weaned gradually as the patient recovers. These may at times all be discontinued within a few weeks to a few months after recovery, sometimes leaving the patient on a lifelong mood stabilizer (like Depakote or Neurontin) and antidepressant (like Wellbutrin-SR, Effexor-XR, or Celexa).

## MAJOR DEPRESSION WITH A HISTORY OF BIPOLAR

If you suffer from major depression and have a history of bipolar, unless the mood elevations are extremely mild, the doctor may give a mood stabilizer along with a proper antidepressant to prevent an "overshoot," a leap into a manic episode. Severely depressed patients, especially those who have abused drugs or alcohol, may have a false expectation that the antidepressant will catapult them out of the depression quickly. It's easy to see why people have this misconception. With severe bronchitis or pneumonia, modern powerful new antibiotics can make you feel totally back to normal in a few days.

Not so with antidepressants. At times, they may barely start to improve symptoms in five to ten days and do not reach their peak effect for a few weeks of a daily dose. So when they don't work, it takes some time to switch out of the process. Fortunately, the newer antidepressants work about 80 percent of the time. Which means the bad news is that they don't work perhaps 15 to 30 percent of the time. When they don't work, however, there are other medications to try. Below is a list of popular antidepressants.

*1. Bupropion-SR (Wellbutrin-SR).* We often use the SR (sustained-release) version. It is longer lasting. This one may be less likely to cause the patient to move into a manic episode, so it is often the first choice of many bipolar experts. It also may help in ADHD.

*2. Citalopram (Celexa).* Popular in Europe for years but new in the U.S. in 1998. Overall, it has less side effects. Many times it may help prevent PMS, anxiety, headaches, and chronic pain syndromes.

*3. Paroxetine (Paxil).* A serotonin builder (SSRI), similar to Celexa. Also eliminates obsessive-compulsive disorder.

*4. Fluoxetine (Prozac).* An SSRI like Paxil, with similar benefits. Long half-life makes it good for forgetful patients (especially teens or the elderly).

*5. Sertraline (Zoloft).* Similar to Paxil and Prozac. An excellent SSRI.

*6. Venlafaxine-XR (Effexor-XR).* Excellent antidepressant that builds up norepinephrine like Wellbutrin-SR, may help in

ADHD, and does all the benefits of numbers three, four, and five, so it is one of the best antidepressants available.

7. *Nefazodene (Serzone).* Atypical serotonin builder with no sexual side effects. Helps insomnia and anxiety. One of the best antidepressants available, especially for those with severe insomnia problems.

8. *Mirtazapine (Remeron).* Too sedating for many people, but some need it for insomnia problems. Weight gain is a frequent problem. Helps anxiety.

9. *Fluvoxamine (Luvox).* Helpful for obsessive-compulsive disorder.

If you end up going through the whole list and find nothing that works, then there is another group to choose from, the old tricyclic antidepressants. The tricyclics include amitriptyline (Elavil), disipramine (Norpramin or Pertofrane), imipramine (Tofranil), and nortriptyline (Pamelor).

Finally, the antidepressants are sometimes used in various combinations or with various augmentation agents (lithium, Synthroid, etc.). If none of these works, the next choice is electroconvulsive shock therapy (ECT).

## ECT
Even though modern-day ECT is much safer and more effective than it was thirty years ago, we are still cautious in using it. In fact, we use ECT as a last resort, only when everything else has failed and when the patient is severely psychotic and/or determined to commit suicide. In that case, we have no problem referring the patient to an outside psychiatrist who specializes in ECT and using it to save a life. And it usually does just that. The short-term memory of the adult receiving ECT may be affected, but that is rarely permanent.

## SEASONAL AFFECTIVE DISORDER
As we mentioned way back in Chapter 2, there are some people

who have wonderful summers. Who, when the sun is shining, energetically go to the beach, to pool parties, to ball games— and in general have a great time. Then winter comes, and on the wings of shorter days comes depression. This type of depression is called seasonal affective disorder. If this rings true for you, call your pharmacist or get in touch with the manufacturer below, and order a special light with enough lumens to mimic sunlight:

> The Sun Box Company
> 19217 Orbit Drive
> Gaithersburg, Maryland 20879
> 1-800-548-3968 or (301) 869-5980
> FAX (301) 977-2281
> E-mail: sunbox@aol.com

Thirty minutes a day under one of their lamps during those shorter, darker days, may help with this disorder's symptoms. If it doesn't, then taking a serotonin building antidepressant every day during the fall and winter seasons may help.

## HOSPITALIZATION

Experts in the field of bipolar may recommend the sufferer be hospitalized when any one of the following symptoms is present:

- severe deterioration in self-care

- high risk of violence or suicide

- severe psychosis (delusional to the point where the delusions may influence the patient's behavior)

We may also recommend hospitalization if the patient is so depressed he is unlikely to cooperate with outpatient treatment, or if the patient is mildly psychotic (loses touch with reality).

If a bipolar patient develops a manic, mixed, or hypomanic episode, the experts may recommend hospitalization if the patient exhibited one of the following symptoms or factors:

- mild psychotic symptoms

- impulsive, poor spending decisions, sexual decisions, or business decisions

- impulsive, poor decisions that alienate the patient's family

- current substance abuse

- outpatient cooperation and responsibility seem unlikely

You should also consider hospitalization if one or more of the following problems are present in a depressed-phase bipolar patient, depending on the number and severity of the problems:

- a past history of at least one severe manic episode, and this is the first significant depressive episode

- one or two trials of outpatient therapy have not brought about an adequate recovery

- a history of rapid cycling (four or more hypomanic or manic episodes per year)

- poor medical health in general

- poor psychosocial support

- exhibiting behavior that is alienating family members

- current substance abuse (alcohol, illegal drugs, or addictive prescription drugs)

Many experts would also consider hospitalization for bipolars who are manic, mixed, or hypomanic, depending on the number and severity of the following problems:

- It is the patient's first manic episode

- There is a history of rapid cycling

- The patient is in poor general health

- Dyphoric mania (mixed depression and mania)

- On an outpatient basis, the patient has been tried on one or two mood stabilizers and is having this current episode anyway

- This patient had never been treated before and the doctor would feel safer treating the patient in a hospital setting

The estimated length of a hospital stay for the bipolar mania or depression is about one to three weeks. This includes the ten days of medication and quiet rest to "come down" from a manic episode before any meaningful psychotherapy. The patient should remain in the hospital until all dangerous ideas and behaviors, psychosis, or disorganized, inappropriate behaviors pass.

## DAY TREATMENT PROGRAMS

If a bipolar patient is moving into a depressive, manic, or hypo-manic phase, but is not a danger to himself or others, then that patient may be able to attend a day program for six hours a day, providing there is close supervision either in a hotel or home by relatives or close friends during the other eighteen hours.

Of course, the patient would have to be healthy enough to participate in group therapy and other day program activities. The psychiatrist would see the patient daily to adjust medications and give reassurance that "this, too, will pass."

After improvement, the bipolar patient can go on to intensive outpatient therapy. This would include daily individual and/or group therapy sessions and fifteen- to thirty-minute medication checks by a psychiatrist three to five days per week for up to several weeks, until the patient is well enough to return to normal functioning. The patient may be monitored on an outpatient basis thereafter for as long as is needed.

If the bipolar patient has a history of rapid cycling, or troubling symptoms in between relapses, or has trouble functioning at home or at work, this outpatient time would be a "severe course." There would be weekly medications management and frequent psychotherapy as needed (individual or group) with a psychiatrist or, possibly, with a qualified non-M.D.

A "moderate course" implies the patient has some difficulty functioning, bipolar episodes every two years or less, and some persistent low-grade symptoms or flare-ups between episodes. For moderate-course treatment, only medication is recommended (after an initial course of therapy is completed).

With the medications currently in use at the beginning of this new millennium, psychiatrists can keep one-third of bipolar patients symptom free for their entire lives. That was the life Brenda enjoyed. After the meds took effect, her cyclothymia quieted, and as long as she keeps taking them, the expectation is that it will remain quiet. Like Brenda, most sufferers will have much fewer and significantly milder episodes of depression, hypomania, mania, or mixed symptoms. New and better medications are being created every year.

## Beyond Medication

With a lifelong genetic life-disturbance like a bipolar disorder, it makes a lot of sense to become an expert on the disorder. In that way, as new medications become available and new treatment methods are developed, you and your family will be able to take advantage of them. How do you become an expert? You read research articles, keep up with changes on the Internet, and have your church elders and deacons pray for you—God is the ultimate physician.

Another thing you might do is join groups committed to keeping abreast of current developments in bipolar research. Depressive and Manic-Depressive Association is one such group, and there are others.

Earlier in this book we presented some guidelines to happiness and keys to spiritual renewal to help you lay a foundation for a more balanced, God-fearing, stress-reduced life. Here are a few more suggestions you might consider.

- Go to bed about the same time every night and wake up naturally when your body says it's time. Of course, you probably have to get up for work and use an alarm clock to make sure you do. Another alternative is to go to bed early enough so you wake up naturally before the alarm goes off. You build up your serotonin while you sleep.

- Attend the church of your choice regularly. Give your life meaning beyond the rat race.

- Bipolars tend to work too hard. Pace yourself, balance your time, take time to smell the roses. Jesus refers to His light burden—take it up.

- Avoid alcohol and illicit drugs altogether. They deplete serotonin and norepinephrine and cause depression. Alcoholics and drug abusers commit suicide seven times more often than others.

- Explain your disorder honestly and openly to your closest family members and friends and ask for their prayers and emotional support—and their help, if appropriate. Don't be embarrassed for having a bipolar disorder any more than other genetic disorders like diabetes or high cholesterol.

- Consider explaining your disorder to your employer so that he or she will know what to expect. Bipolar employees tend to be better employees because there are times (most of the time) when they can cram twelve hours' work into eight. But they also have slower times. And their employers should understand their work rhythm.

- Keep a "mood journal" and put a few brief comments in it every night before you go to bed.

By following these few suggestions, what you have learned in Parts 1 through 3 of this book will be enhanced.

You are probably reading this book because you or one of your loved ones have not been happy with life because of moods and mood swings. Medication is an important ingredient in changing all that. So, it becomes imperative that you take your meds—that you get yourself on a schedule and take them faithfully. If you don't, you're courting disaster. Within a few weeks, or if you're fortunate, a few months of abandoning them, you will be back where you started—except worse.

Perhaps even in the hospital.

You would think that a person faced with that prospect would put taking medication as the first item on their to-do list. Not so. Psychiatrists have actually composed a list of the most frequently quoted reasons bipolars neglect to take their medication:

- I was feeling fine, so I quit my meds.

- They are expensive.

- They are a hassle.

- They are a stigma.

- I miss the highs. My business does better and I feel better when I'm high.

- The meds keep me too "normal," too boring.

- I don't like the side effects.

Take your medication. Enlist others to hold you accountable.

One of our clients asked three different people to call him once a week to make sure he takes his meds. Another has his wife place the medication next to his breakfast plate and stare at him until he downs it. If you're prone to neglect things, come up with a way of making sure you don't neglect this. It could mean life or death, since 10 percent of bipolars commit suicide, often during a totally unnecessary manic or depressive episode that could have been avoided by faithfully taking their medications.

In the next chapter, we will discuss some additional things you might do to help manage your wellness and a few things your family can do not only to help you in times of crisis, but to protect themselves from injury when things go a little off kilter.

# 16 Managing Your Emotional Wellness

The first thing to come to grips with when managing your wellness is to understand that you may be dealing with a lifelong issue—a genetic disorder. No surgery will cure it, nor will any medication. The only thing that will keep it at bay and minimize its effects on you and your family is to put attitudes, methods, and proper medication in place to manage it.

From now on you need to live a life that minimizes the external influences that can cause mood swings, that maximizes the effects of the medication, and that keeps the damage done by any recurrences to a bare minimum.

We have already discussed at length ways to order your life to attack the external influences, and we have discussed the importance of faithfully taking your medication and even given you a few suggestions on how you might make sure you do that. Now let's go on to the final element: putting the attitudes and methods in place to make sure any recurrences cause as little upset as possible.

## THE "MOOD JOURNAL"

Dr. Minirth sat across from Wendy. Autumn was coming to the Dallas area and there was a crisp bite in the air. To thwart it,

233

Wendy wore a thick, fall-colored sweater and sleek brown pants. A few months before she had come there talking a mile a minute and fidgeting uncontrollably, now she looked wonderfully calm and at ease.

"A mood journal." She repeated the words.

"Although you seem to be doing pretty well," Dr. Minirth said, "bipolar II isn't anything to take for granted."

"I'm really no good at keeping journals," Wendy said. "I tried to keep a diary in high school once. Frankly, the time I took to write things down kept me from doing things I wanted to put in there."

"This is not that kind of book. You're not trying to write down everything you did during the day. Only certain things. And reading it later is not for enjoyment. It's to help you keep track of how you feel in relationship to stressful events in your life. It's also to get you to check your moods so that if you're on the ragged edge of a coming depression or hypomanic episodes, you'll know it and come in for help."

"Okay," Wendy nodded. "You convinced me. What do I put in this mood journal?"

"First thing to remember: whatever you write, write in complete sentences so it's clear if you have to read it back. Now, what to write. Your overall mood during the day—rating it between zero to ten, ten being the most manic, zero being the most depressed. It's also helpful to note what might have led to a change in mood. Also, note any changes in sleep patterns, energy levels, if you have any thoughts about death, sudden optimism, whether you begin dressing more fetchingly, any unusual sexual fantasies, changes in self-esteem, and, of course, any significant moods that might arise. Get your husband's input too. Often he will notice things before you do. And take particular note of your sleeping patterns. Changes can be an early warning. Just a couple of sentences a day will do."

"What then?" she asked.

"If your moods break out of what you consider normal, either too high or too low, or if your sleep pattern or energy level changes appreciably, come in and see me. Actually, there are a number of reasons to come in. If you have any suicidal feelings, I want you in here or at least on the phone the instant you have them. I don't want to lose you—we've been working together too long. Although you've never had them, if you have any violent feelings, get on the phone with me. Or if you notice anything that might be a new side effect of the medication.

"Another thing you need to keep in mind. Because you're taking bipolar meds, if you become ill or need surgery or any extensive dental care, especially if you need to take any new medications, let me know. We don't want your bipolar meds affected. You might want to carry a little notebook and pencil around with you. Jot down anything that contributes to a major mood swing as it occurs, so you don't forget."

## YOUR OWN MOOD JOURNAL

The last thing an emotional-health professional wants to do is load up a patient with homework. You don't have a lot of time and energy in your busy life, and if you don't do the homework, then guilt may stand in the way of coming to see the professional when you should. So our asking you to do this shows you how important it is.

A key to managing your wellness is keeping a heads-up for any changes. By recognizing the onset of any new episode, medications can be strengthened, your support group can be alerted, and you can take precautions so that you can prevent the episode from occurring at all, or minimize the impact of the episode if it does occur.

Keeping the journal, along with taking your meds, is essential to a sound management program. Another important aspect of your recovery is getting the most out of your therapy sessions.

The most important thing about therapy is your attitude. Psychotherapy is vital to relieving the stresses that can trigger depressive or manic episodes. Do not neglect your therapy, even if there are times when you think you're spending too much money. You're not. The alternative is to spend that money, and probably far more, going through difficult mood episodes.

And since it is so important, do not see a therapist who belittles you or your spiritual values. Rather, find one who will encourage the things you deem important and help you discover new ways to find strength and stamina from them. You want someone who is smart, knowledgeable, but also compassionate, spiritual, and biblical.

Just as finding the right therapist is important, knowing when you need help is also important. You will find you need far more therapy and medication management while tunneling through a depressive period than you do during a manic or hypomanic episode (things are just too hectic). But you also want to keep your counselor (psychiatrist) informed when you're moving through normalcy. A good time to do that is during your medication management visit every few months.

If you are heading into a particularly stressful period, you may want to meet with your counselor more often for a while. But in any case, don't be bashful about asking for help and taking advantage of the help that's there. You will not need to see your therapist weekly for the rest of your life.

Now that you know you have bipolar II and are on the road to feeling normal again, see the therapist for six months to a year on a weekly basis. Learn everything you can about yourself, how your childhood affects you, and what stresses you out. Learn better boundaries and communication skills with your spouse, kids, and friends. Learn about your own mood swings. Then quit your therapy sessions, unless you start going into a depressive dip or a hypomanic breakthrough. If you do, see the therapist again once or twice a week until the crisis is past. Then quit again. Expect to hear your psychiatrist say, "Come see me for fifteen minutes once every three months just so I can check on your meds and ask you a few key symptom-type questions. But call me or my nurse any time you have a med question or significant symptoms." Sound easy enough?

## COUNSELING TECHNIQUES

Psychological help comes by way of various counseling techniques. There's behavioral therapy—focusing on stress-reducing behaviors (i.e. getting enough sleep, setting boundaries). And cognitive therapy, which (pardon the use of the word) stresses positive thinking and dealing with emotions through training your thought processes and learning realistic optimism. Interpersonal therapy deals with communication styles and improving relationships. And eclectic therapy uses all three approaches, depending on the situation.

We focus on the eclectic approach, and we are insight-oriented. This therapy asks our patients to understand their own areas of codependency (faulty people-to-people habits and over-dependencies) and the underlying emotional issues that have supported their lives all the way from childhood to the present. No matter which techniques are being used, you always need to be honest and vulnerable with the therapist and completely yourself. Think out loud, feel out loud. Never just try to please your therapist or fear that he or she might reject you. And if you find yourself fearing the therapist or being intimidated, tell him. And never, never play head games in therapy—it's serious business. Therapy is truly one of the only things you can do that exercises your mind, your emotions, and your spirituality—and works to bring them all into harmony.

## FLAVORS OF THERAPY

Therapy comes in several flavors—individual, marital, family, and group—and all have their proper time and place. They also come with various time schedules and intensities—outpatient, intensive outpatient, day treatment, or inpatient hospitalization (voluntary or when committed). And in all its varieties and intensities, therapy is a slow, gradual process that builds on itself over time. It may take years—and it may be sporadic with "on" times and "off."

But no matter how it unfolds for you personally, the benefits are lifelong to both you and your descendants and their descendants too. When you become more emotionally balanced, those who depend on you for emotional support, your children for instance, turn out more emotionally balanced as well.

## YOUR SUPPORT GROUP

Wendy looked perplexed. "I know I should bring Peter into all this," Wendy said. "After all, he's been in this from the beginning. But I don't know about the rest of my family."

"You don't have to bring everyone into the inner circle. Only three or four you completely trust. The rest of your family—those you socialize with—should know you have this problem that you're taking medication to control, and that your bipolar disorder can cause you to act erratically at times. You want to let them know that, like any wild animal in captivity, your disorder might break free one day. Maybe you left the gate open by not watching your moods well enough, or maybe it just jumps the fence. So if they see you behaving in a hypomanic way, they are not to take it personally, but they're to tell Peter, or some other member of your support group. Then they're to keep you in check, or at least keep an eye on you, until the cavalry arrives. That cavalry is your support group—three or four people who love you and whom you trust to make sound decisions."

"Like my mom, and Jean (we've been friends since high school), and my cousin, Les. Great guy. Good Christian man."

## BUILDING YOUR OWN SUPPORT GROUP

Initially, it is probably best to choose people within your immediate family. Even if they are critical at times, they're wonderful people who always love you. Pick three or four you're closest to, strong people who are able to make difficult decisions. Go to them individually at first, telling them about your problem. Even if they know about it already, tell them everything you've learned and what your current situation is. Then tell them what you want them to do—we'll cover that in a moment. Having them over as a group, after that initial contact, is a good idea. Even though they probably already know each other intimately, they need to come together with you about this issue. You will be surprised and gratified at how quickly they begin working together to make sure that, whatever happens, you're taken care of. However, if a member of the group doesn't seem to fit in, or in some way looks like he doesn't belong, gently, kindly, lovingly, tell him so. Then replace him with someone more appropriate.

Now, what does your support group do?

Your support group is your first line of defense against the full-blown recurrence of your disorder. To act in that capacity the group needs to be willing to do a number of things.

- They must be willing to discuss your disorder with you without being judgmental or condescending. Their attitude must be one of respect and a willingness to help. If it's not, tell them lovingly that it should be.

239

- They need to educate themselves about the disorder. Just as you have, they must read this book and other relevant materials, becoming well-versed on the symptoms, causes, and control of mood swings.

- It's good for them to attend a meeting with your psychiatrist or counselor during one of your medication management visits. This gives the group and the counselor a chance to meet, and it gives the counselor additional information about your behavior—things you may not have noticed or forgotten.

- While you're "normal," make a plan with your support group, complete with any necessary documents, that covers what your wishes are if you should become manic or suicidal. (See the sample Crisis Plan in this chapter.) Your plan should include everything necessary for your involuntary commitment and any waivers necessary to allow a mental health-care professional to administer what's needed to keep you from harming yourself or others. When you are mentally incapacitated, you want those closest to you to be able to make these life-sustaining decisions. Then make sure that each member of your support group has copies of everything.

---

### Crisis Plan for (insert your name)

When I am feeling well, I am (describe yourself when you are feeling well):

The following symptoms indicate that I am no longer able to make decisions for myself, that I am no longer able to be responsible for myself.

When I clearly have some of the above symptoms, I want the following people to make decisions for me, to see that I get appropriate treatment, and to give me care and support.

I do not want the following people involved in any way in my care or treatment. List names and (optional) why you do not want them involved.

Preferred medications and why:

Acceptable medications and why:

Unacceptable medications and why:

Acceptable treatments and why:

Unacceptable treatments and why:

Preferred treatment facilities and why:

Unacceptable treatment facilities and why:

What I want from my support group when I am experiencing these symptoms:

What I do not want from my support group when I am experiencing these symptoms:

Things I need others to do for me and who I want to do them:

How I want disagreements between my supports settled:

Things I can do for myself:

I (give, do not give) permission for my supports to talk with each other about my symptoms and to make plans on how to assist me.

I developed this document myself with the help and support of:

Signed: _____    Date: _____

Attorney: _____    Date: _____

Witness: _____    Date: _____

Witness: _____    Date: _____

- Pray with members of your support group as often as you can. Pray *for* them, that God might somehow reward them for making this extra effort in your life. Pray for yourself, that you might be equipped to handle all the stress in your life, and that, if an episode should come, God will be right there with you. And pray for your psychiatrist and your counselor. Pray that God gives them wisdom and stamina, not only in your case, but in all their cases, and that they might have the opportunity to point their patients in the right direction—physically, emotionally, and spiritually.

- Always speak the truth to one another in love. That goes two ways. If there are issues you have with certain members of your support group, talk about them—and resolve them—in love. And be prepared to hear the truth from them, particularly if you are not taking your meds. We hope you hear about that again and again until you start taking them faithfully. And if they tell you a mood is on the way, listen to them and react accordingly. They will often perceive things you haven't yet noticed.

## Setting Boundaries

This section is written both for the bipolar sufferer and his or her family.

A boundary is simply an emotional and physical line that defines you as a person. It defines what you're responsible for and what you're not. By knowing your boundaries, you can put plans in place and take actions that fulfill those responsibilities, keeping watch over them to make sure all is and remains well within your boundaries. After all, these are your God-given responsibilities. Responsibilities like your emotional and physical health, your family, your job, your talents and gifts. And since they are God-given, you have also been given access to all the tools necessary to fulfill them.

Right away you can see how properly defining your boundaries can reduce your levels of stress. It is far less stressful to work on things over which you have reasonable control and the tools you need than it is to take on responsibility for something over which you have limited or no control and few, if any, tools.

Here are some suggestions for setting boundaries.

- Realize that your emotional health is every bit as important as the emotional health of those you're dealing with. Of course, there may be times when you do need to make physical and emotional sacrifices, but unless it is a true emergency, one involving life and death, you should never put your emotional or physical well-being at risk.

- Respect the property of others—all that resides within their boundaries, all they are responsible for, both physically and emotionally. This means that you behave in a way that communicates you in no way want to come between them and their need to fulfill the responsibilities God has given them. You don't want to take too much of their time, their attention, or their energy. You don't want to cause them any stress that might curtail their ability to perform. Actually, the opposite is true. Where possible, you want to help them take care of their property. You want to be part of their solution and certainly not part of their problem.

- Do not take on any responsibility that rightfully belongs to another if:

  - you lack reasonable control over it

  - you lack the necessary tools to accomplish it

  - you have a personal need that will not get accomplished because of it

  - by taking the responsibility on you are enabling the other person to shirk responsibility or to continue to manage his or her life poorly. Keep in mind, you're doing no one a favor by encouraging that.

- Do not take responsibility for another person's mistakes. You may want to lend a hand, but feel free to turn the task back to them anytime you think you're being taken advantage of. We all make mistakes, and it seems somehow callous to refuse to help when someone is suffering from one of theirs. After all, you would want someone's help in the same situation. But mistakes are often the result of poor planning and management. Don't find yourself being someone's perpetual backstop. Rather, it's better for him, and you, to help him to a place where he doesn't need one. Saying a loving "no" can do that.

- Remember, a request for assistance is just that, a request, and you should not get upset if you get a "no" answer. And you should not feel guilty if you give a "no" answer. You both have lives to live, and only a certain amount of time and energy to live them. Special requests eat into that time. Life is too stressful as it is without trying to cram two lives into the space of one. However, if you do have the time and energy, and all other conditions we have discussed before are met, why not help?

- Doing something for someone should never be a condition of giving or receiving love. Implied in a lot of people's requests for help is the threat that if help is refused, love will be withdrawn. That's a terrible choice to face. When we respect the other person's property—respect the other person's need to fulfill his or her responsibilities—we also must love them when they make choices whose ultimate aim is, indeed, to fulfill those responsibilities. Therefore, whether they help us or not should be immaterial to our love.

- If you take responsibility for something and suddenly the situation changes mid-project, rethink and renegotiate—and if appropriate, give the project back. We have all had situations like this. A bipolar loved one asks for help dropping off a few of his shirts, too, since you're on your way to the cleaners. You agree, but when you arrive he has a whole list of chores for you to do—go to the market, drop off some papers to be copied. Suddenly a nothing kind of favor becomes an all-afternoon event.

You owe it to your responsibilities to stop at that moment and consider this new situation as you would a whole new request—a request subject to all the criteria of a new request. And at that point it's perfectly okay to say "no" to all the new stuff.

- If you lend a hand in an emergency that is clearly the other person's fault, counsel the person afterward about getting his life in order so future emergencies are avoided. If the person fails to take the necessary steps, then you may have to let him know that the next time he's on his own. It is very hard not to help in an emergency. Of course, unless the emergency is life or death, the term can become subjective. What is an emergency to you may not be one to me. So if these emergencies happen more often than seems reasonable—and frankly, emergencies don't happen that often—you need to do whatever is practical to your way of thinking to help the person get his life in order, then let his new system work.

- Take care not to be manipulated. Guilt can be a strong motivator and many people know that. They have developed ways of playing on our guilt like Isaac Stern plays his Stradivarius. Be careful. If you are doing something out of guilt, just don't do it. That is the wrong reason to do anything. Do it out of love. Do it out of duty. Do it because you simply have nothing better to do. But don't do it out of guilt. If the person is playing on your guilt, he or she is no true friend—and tell the person so. And then examine your guilt and discover why it's there. False guilt comes from the idea that you should be doing something you're not. Or you shouldn't be doing something you are doing. If you shouldn't be doing it, don't—and if you should be doing it, do. And if you shouldn't be feeling guilty about it in the first place, stop. If you have trouble doing any of this, seek help. False guilt only adds to stress, and we have too much of that around already. True guilt when we sin is good, but false guilt is a ball and chain around our necks.

By taking these steps lovingly and consciously, you will set up a relational environment that will not only help diminish the levels of stress but also help everyone take care of their responsibilities in a far more loving and effective way.

In this chapter, we have described how to set up and manage your journey through wellness. By following these suggestions, by working to get the most out of therapy, and by setting up and working within your own boundaries while respecting the boundaries of others, you will be well on the way to living an exciting, fulfilled life for yourself, your loved ones, and for the Lord, with the least amount of stress on your life.

In the final chapter, we will take the bipolar's family aside and discuss some things that are important for them.

# 17

## A WORD FOR THE FAMILIES
## OF BIPOLAR SUFFERERS

We want to address this chapter to the support group members and any other interested, caring members of the bipolar's family. We are assuming that you have read this entire book, particularly the section just before this. If you haven't, please do.

You have a brave person in your family. Many people suffering from bipolar spectrum disorders simply self-medicate with alcohol or drugs and never come in for help. Many of those who come in never complete the process, reverting back to their moods and mood swings before reaching wellness—the journey was just too difficult, took too much discipline. However, your loved one is daring to do the difficult—he or she is actually doing the emotional and physical work necessary to be well. What the sufferer is doing takes courage and commitment. So congratulate him or her.

As a member of that person's family, you can do a number of things to help. First, encourage your loved one. Encourage him to talk to you about the disorder, about how it's affecting his life, and what's going on in his life right now. And especially encourage him to talk to you if there is ever a problem he needs help solving—even if it has nothing to do with the disorder. By helping him solve life issues, you are reducing his level of stress, which helps him manage the disorder.

But a word of caution about this. You, too, need to protect yourself. Your loved one's requests for help should be reasonable requests. What is reasonable? Only you can say, but essentially, reasonable requests are for things you're willing to give. If you find yourself being taken advantage of, put a halt to it. By doing so you will force your loved one to do a better job of managing. Encourage him to stick with the program—to stay on the medication, see his psychiatrist regularly (feel free to come with him to a session or two if his psychiatrist says it's okay), avoid alcohol and drugs, get a second opinion if needed, and generally help him eliminate any unnecessary stress in his life.

What if your loved one has a mood episode and becomes hostile or hard to manage? If she should suddenly turn on you and begin to abuse you verbally—calling you "interfering," or "only in the way," or something else abusive instead of thanking you for keeping your promise to care—make sure you remind yourself that it is a biochemical reaction talking and not your loved one. For the moment, she is being held captive against her will. Don't take it personally. She will apologize later.

In fact, it's a good idea, particularly if you are the spouse of the sufferer, to have a plan to deal with these more extreme situations when they occur. Although every setting is different, you should consider for your plan the following:

- taking away all credit cards—a manic or hypomanic person can easily spend the entire life's savings in an hour.

- having legal control over his or her banking privileges—e.g., a requirement for two signatures.

- taking away car keys during a mood episode.

- hospitalization whenever the sufferer is out of control, even if he or she refuses.

As you can see, this task can be difficult, and the only thing that makes a load lighter is to share it. We always encourage bipolars to bring together a support group to help share the family burden, but sometimes they ignore that advice. If your loved one has, then it falls on you to bring together caring people willing to share the task. And when you do, rather than thinking about this as a burden, think of it as an opportunity to feel good about yourself for being a quality person who is willing to help someone you truly love. As the song says, "He ain't heavy. He's my brother."

## REALISTIC EXPECTATIONS

During the recovery stages from a mood episode, try to have realistic expectations. Your loved one will probably not be able to go to work full-time right away. He or she may have to increase the workload gradually. On the other hand, don't expect him to be an invalid, either. He just had a difficult experience, but not a permanently debilitating one. There is no need to be overprotective. Do things with your loved one, not for him. And most important, unless he is in an acute episode, do not make decisions for him. He needs the self-respect that comes from as much self-reliance as is reasonable and possible. When he is recovering from an episode, treat him normally. Remember, we all have good days and bad days. And even though you want to be on the lookout for recurrence, don't overinterpret every good day as hypomanic and every bad one as a depression.

Speaking of depressions, sad times will come. We all have them. A pet dies, a dream fades. So when your loved one is sad, encourage him or her to cry—just as you encourage yourself. Sadness is a part of reality, and relieving it restores joy to life.

And finally, let your loved one take care of you now and again. Not only physically, but emotionally. It is condescending to be the caretaker all the time. Share some of your own difficult times with him or her and let your loved one give you advice and help you through the valley.

## YOU NEED SUPPORT TOO

Find your own support group. Either through a special interest group, or through church. Let other people love you and encourage you, just as you're loving and giving encouragement. And the greatest support you can get is from God. Pray as often as you can and allow the Holy Spirit to buoy you and carry you through.

Finally, a word about suicide.

## ISSUES SURROUNDING SUICIDE

Bipolars have a higher suicide rate than others. This means two things. First, what you're doing is important for your loved one. Someday you might actually be saving his life, so please be vigilant and serious about your responsibilities to him. It also means that one day your loved one might take his own life. It's a horrible thing to contemplate, and we suggest you not dwell on it at all. Instead, dwell on the positive.

But since suicide is a real possibility, there is one thing we want you to keep in mind: you cannot keep anyone alive but yourself. You may do all the right things, be there every time he needs you, say all the things you believe to be supportive, and he still might commit suicide. If he does, grieve his loss—grieve it deeply—and shed equally deep and cleansing tears as you let out your sadness. But do not hang on to it and do not let destructive feelings of guilt and shame take over. It was not your responsibility to keep your loved one alive. That was between him and God. No one else. You only agreed to love him and "speak the truth in love" to him. That's all.

That said, it is still imperative that you learn the warning signs of suicide so you can speak competently about your concerns if the need arises. Those warning signs include the following.

*1. Suicide threats.* If he begins threatening suicide, or talking as if he has already decided to do it, take everything he says seriously.

*2. Suicide gestures.* If he cuts himself superficially or overdoses on a few aspirins, or does anything else that looks like a rehearsal or a test to see how it might feel, intervene. Ten percent of people who make these kinds of superficial gestures *do* commit suicide later.

*3. Getting things in order.* If he begins to get his affairs in order—taking care of his will, adding to life insurance, gathering things together so they can be easily found, summing up relationships, maybe getting closure on people he hasn't seen in years, maybe even saying good-bye to them or doing anything that looks as if he is preparing for death—that's exactly what he's doing.

*4. Increased expressions of despair.* He speaks of how miserable he is and how he will never feel any better. "The grave has to be better than this." He's talking himself into it, giving himself a reason for committing suicide and telling you what that reason is. He wants you to understand.

If you see these behaviors unfolding and, after speaking with your loved one, the behaviors continue and you get to the point where you honestly believe a suicide attempt is coming, you have to act. Here are some things you should consider doing.

- Call 911 if his situation becomes desperate.

- Call his psychiatrist and do whatever the psychiatrist tells you to do.

- Reassure him that his suicide would not be a relief—that's what he's probably thinking—but rather it would be a great personal loss and a burden to all his loved ones.

- Get him to sit down and read Chapter 5 in this book—the suicide prevention chapter.

- Do not allow yourself to be manipulated if he turns on you or gives you false promises or has a phony "flight" back to emotional health. Do not assume things are better. His psychiatrist or some other mental health-care professional should be the one to pronounce the crisis over.

- If appropriate, carry out the prepared crisis plan when your loved one goes into a manic or hypomanic episode, or remains dangerous to himself or others—including commitment, if necessary.

Loving, supporting, and caring for the needs of a bipolar sufferer can be quite challenging, as you have seen. But the situation is far from hopeless. We trust the resources in this book will help you and your loved one learn to live victoriously with this genetic disorder. With the proper medication and counseling, most bipolar patients will achieve significant improvement. And for those who need extra psychiatric attention or counseling, help is available. If you cannot find a Christian counselor in your area, call one of our clinics and we will try to refer you to a qualified therapist. (Information on how to contact us is located at the back of this book.)

We leave you with this brief reminder of the advice we have offered for coping with a bipolar disorder: Encourage your loved one to take the prescribed medication faithfully. Seek qualified Christian counseling. Set boundaries. Try to minimize external influences that cause stress. Rely on the support group you have built. And, above all, rely on our Wonderful Counselor, Mighty God, Everlasting Father, Prince of Peace—Jesus Christ (Isa. 9:6 NIV)—to give you the humility to accept your genetic disorder and the courage and strength to follow the many steps in this book. May His grace and peace be yours.

# DEPRESSION, MEDICINE, AND FIFTY-TWO HYPOTHETICAL CASES

"Is there no balm in Gilead,
Is there no physician there?" (Jer. 8:22 NIV)

There are Christian physicians today, and the tools God has given them (including medicine) can be remarkable in the healing process.

Depressive disorders are more prevalent than heart disease and cancer combined, and the annual economic cost for depression is more than for heart disease. The recognition of heart disease and cancer is high while the recognition of depression remains low. The treatment outcome of heart disease and cancer is variable while the treatment outcome for depression in general is good.

The question should be "How can one be the most effective for Christ?"

## WHY TREAT?

If depression and bipolar disorders are not treated, they may become more resistant to treatment later.

It is important to realize the genetic elements described previously. Depressions and bipolar disorders run in families. In fact, it may be that bipolar disorders carry a more genetic load than any other mental disorder. It is also important to note that stressors will precede a bipolar mood swing; therefore, stress needs to be reduced.

Effectiveness for Christ is an extremely important issue. If medication is used appropriately to decrease symptoms and allows one to be functional for Christ, then it should be considered.

## Which Antidepressant to Use?

There are many factors to consider when deciding which antidepressant to use. Below are some general thoughts and considerations.

Dr. Minirth attends as many psychopharmacology conferences as he can each year. By meeting with the top specialists in the world in the field, Dr. Minirth prides himself on being current and well-informed on the latest medication. Below is some of the latest thinking in this field. The hypothetical cases listed here are based on some of the latest thinking in this field at the time the book was printed.

Decisions always must be decided on a case-by-case basis. One factor that may be considered is the possible side effects, both desirable and undesirable. Chemicals in the brain (neurotransmitters) often play a role in side effects. Not only do we know today which neurotransmitters produce which side effects (weight gain, sleep, pain, calmness, etc.), we even know many subdivisions of one neurotransmitter. Many times we can target the side effect and the results. This has become a science in and of itself known as psychopharmacology.

The following are hypothetical cases. Again, the answers are simply general thoughts and are not meant to replace individual decisions made by local doctors who have the facts. Also, psychopharmacology is changing at an unbelievably rapid rate. What is used today may change tomorrow.

## Fifty-Two Hypothetical Cases

1. Client has depression and ADHD: Wellbutrin-SR, Effexor-XR.

2. Client has depression and wants less sexual side effects: Wellbutrin-SR, Remeron, or possibly Serzone.

3. Client has depression, anxiety, and insomnia: Remeron, Serzone.

4. Client has depression and anxiety: Effexor-XR or Serzone.

5. Client is depressed and does not want to gain weight: Wellbutrin-SR, possibly Effexor-XR, Serzone.

6. Client is depressed and wants to gain weight: Remeron.

7. Client is depressed and has Alzeheimer's dementia: Wellbutrin-SR plus Aricept.

8. Client is depressed and has much anger: SSRIs such as Prozac, Paxil, Zoloft.

9. Client is depressed but has a past history of a manic episode. He is already on Lithium and wants to know if an additional drug might help: Wellbutrin-SR.

10. Client is depressed with a bipolar history, is on antidepressant Wellbutrin-SR but also has anxiety, social phobia, neutrogenic pain, obsessive worry, insomnia and/or alcohol/benzodiazepine addiction: Neurontin.

11. Client is depressed, is on an antidepressant, has a history of abuse of benzodiazepines (valium, etc.) in the past, but has a lot of ongoing anxiety: BuSpar.

12. Client has a mild depression and absolutely refuses a standard antidepressant, but says he is going to take an herb because it is "natural": St. John's Wort. It is dangerous with MAO inhibitors.

13. Client is depressed but somewhat paranoid and perhaps has some almost psychotic-like symptoms: Zyprexa, Risperdal, or Seroquel.

14. Client has a severe psychotic depression but has a movement disorder (Tardive dyskinesia) from past old antipsychotic drugs: Zyprexa (new atypical antipsychotic) plus vitamin E perhaps.

15. Client is now manic with major depressions in the past: Depakote, Lithium, Tegretol or Neurontin.

16. Client is on a mood stabilizer but still not stable and needs an additional medicine: Neurontin, Lamictal.

17. Client is on a mood stabilizer but is having an acute psychotic flare: Zyprexa, Risperdal, or Seroquel.

18. Client wants a drug with a tendency to low interactions with many other medicines: Celexa (even here caution should be used—it should not be used for example with MAO inhibitors or propulsed).

19. A depressed client who also has high blood pressure but is on no medicine for the high blood pressure: Celexa plus Visken (may cause a more rapid response of the antidepressant).

20. A depressed female who has severe PMS: Zoloft.

21. Client is depressed but also has obsessive worries: Prozac, Paxil, or Zoloft.

22. Client is depressed and also has panic disorder: Prozac, Paxil, Zoloft, Xanax is more addicting than Klonopin, but either can be used prn or in regular doses until the antidepressant relieves the panic disorder in 2–10 weeks, then the addicting benzodiazepine (Klonopin or Xanax) can be gradually weaned away or saved for panic attacks.

23. Client is depressed and has not responded to an antidepressant alone: Cytomel (thyroid), estrogen (possible cancer side effects), beta blocker (Visken).

24. Client is in good health and has responded well to an SSRI (Prozac, Paxil, Zoloft) but has sexual side effects: Wellbutrin-SR, addition Viagra prn.

25. A depressed client says he heard how great the SSRI antidepressants are but wants one that may possibly be less prone to sexual side effects: Wellbutrin-SR, Remeron or Serzone.

26. A depressed client wants help as quickly as possible: possibly Celexa or Remeron.

27. A depressed client has been resistant to antidepressants. She is tired in the day and can't sleep at night: Wellbutrin-SR, Remeron. Desyrel can also be used with Wellbutrin-SR to help females fall asleep, but is best avoided in men because of potential priapism, possibly requiring surgery.

28. An SSRI has been helping but the depression remains: SSRI plus Wellbutrin-SR (which is the same drug as Zyban).

29. The depressed client also wants to stop smoking: Wellbutrin-SR.

30. The depressed client has liver disease: Celexa—eliminated more by the kidney.

31. Client is depressed and has a sexual addiction: Prozac.

32. Client was depressed, responded well to an SSRI, also has a problem with impotence due to other medical issues: Viagra.

33. Client is depressed, emaciated and very self-conscious about her physical appearence: Prozac.

34. Client is depressed, somewhat emaciated appearing, and is considering breast augmentation: Prozac.

35. Client is bipolar but has not responded very well to Depakote, Lithium, Tegretol, and Neurontin. There is a history of a lot of depression in his past: Lamictal/Lamotrigine (concerns with rare Stevens-Johnson Syndrome).

36. Client is bipolar, has a history of seizures, is not adequately controlled with Depakote alone, desires to lose weight: Topamax/Topiramate).

37. Client is in an acute manic (mood stabilizers started) phase and needs sleep: Klonopin, Zyprexa.

38. Client is in an acute manic state, has a movement disorder (TD) from use of Thorazine in the past, is not responding to mood stabilizers, is plainly psychotic: Zyprexa.

39. Client is a child with ADHD but also may have some mild depression: Dexedrine (Adderall and Ritalin are also used in ADHD).

40. Client is depressed, has not responded to most of the antidepressants, and insists on going back on an MAO inhibitor to which he responded well in the past and knows of potentially dangerous drug and food interactions: Nardil, Parnate.

41. Client is depressed and has kidney disease: Celexa.

42. Client is depressed, has extreme obsessive anxious worries, has not responded to Prozac alone, even at 80 mg per day plus Xanax (or Klonopin): Neurontin or BuSpar.

43. Client is depressed, very obsessive, near a psychosis, and has not responded to Prozac alone: Zyprexa.

44. Client is depressed and menopausal: Zoloft plus estrogen and progesterone.

45. Client is depressed and has been on most old tricyclic antidepressants (Tofranil, Elavil, Sinequan, Pamelor, Vivactil, etc., but has had many side effects: Celexa, Wellbutrin-SR.

46. Client is doing well on the Wellbutrin-SR but cannot sleep: Desyrel or Remeron, if female. Remeron, if male.

47. Client is extremely depressed, is pregnant, knows potential risk but says she must have an antidepressant: Wellbutrin-SR or possibly Prozac.

48. Client is depressed and has tried several antidepressants at maximum dosages. Results have been poor. Wellbutrin-SR plus an SSRI (Prozac, Zoloft, Paxil) has not worked and Wellbutrin-SR plus Remeron has not worked: Effexor-XR plus Wellbutrin-SR, Effexor-XR plus Remeron. (One does well to watch for serotonin

syndrome if both drugs that block serotonin are being used at the same time).

49. Client is depressed and has tried several antidepressants at maximum dosages. Results have been poor. Wellbutrin-SR plus an SSRI (Prozac, Zoloft, Paxil) has not worked and Wellbutrin-SR plus Remeron has not worked: Celexa plus Wellbutrin-SR.

50. Client is depressed and has tried several antidepressants at maximum dosages. Results have been poor. Wellbutrin-SR plus an SSRI (Prozac, Zoloft, Paxil) has not worked and Wellbutrin-SR plus Remeron has not worked: Effexor-XR plus Celexa. (But watch for Seratonin Syndrome.)

51. Client is depressed and has a history of seizures. The antidepressant *least likely* to be chosen: Wellbutrin.

52. Client is depressed and has a long history of significantly low cell counts of red blood cells, white blood cells, and platelets. The antidepressant perhaps *least likely* to be chosen: Remeron.

## THE HEALTH FOOD STORE AND DEPRESSION

Depressed individuals often say they have visited the health food store and have questioned the claims of many natural remedies including:

- St. John's Wort (Hypericum perforatum) for depression
- KAVA for depression and anxiety
- Omega 3 fatty acids for bipolar disorder
- Inositol for obsessive worry and depression

- Melatonin and Valerian for the insomnia of depression

- "Natural" progesterone for mood stabilization

- Choline (Lecithin) for mood stabilization

- Ginger root for side effects of SSRI withdrawal

- Acidophilus for diarrhea side effects of an antidepressant

- Gingko for SSRI-associated sexual dysfunction

In some cases, herbs may work. Some of these agents probably do not work at all; some probably work by a strong placebo effect; some probably work but are dangerous in uneducated hands.

Natural does not necessarily mean safe. Strychnine, cyanide, and arsenic are also natural but deadly. Self-treatment by clients with natural herbs can be dangerous at times.

Also, dangerous interactions can occur when self-treating: St. John's Wort with an MAO inhibitor antidepressant could kill; KAVA has caused cases of coma when combined with Xanax. Gingko with Coumadin could be dangerous. Ephedra (in many herbal diet pills) alone could be dangerous at times. Inositol could precipitate a manic episode.

These herbs are in general unregulated. How does one know St. John's Wort has three hundred milligrams of hypericum perforatum per pill? The FDA does not control this.

Interesting observations can be made. Some individuals will not trust a medical doctor but will trust someone with limited education at a health food store and take pills that have not been regulated according to the amount of substance in the dose.

Sometimes drugs are not technically approved for a specific use but are used by physicians in the community as a matter of practice or are used because the use makes logical sense. This is the case with many drugs that are used in various mood disorders.

## TOUGH CASES OF MEDICAL DEPRESSION

We often see patients who may appear to have treatment-resistant cases of depression. But every year there is a psychopharmacology conference to help psychiatrists understand the cutting edge of medical treatments for difficult cases.

Below are some of the latest thoughts by some of the best minds in the world in psychopharmacology. However, the decision about which drugs to use for each individual should be made by the local physician.

1. *Antidepressants with other helpful drugs.* There are a number of relatively new antidepressants (Celexa, Effexor-XR, Remeron, and Wellbutrin-SR) that offer great hope and with less side effects overall and, in fact, may offer certain desired side effects such as increased energy, increased focus, etc. Sometimes in tough cases these antidepressants are used in combination or with other augmentation strategies such as the addition of various medication like a beta blocker (Visken), lithium, a thyroid preparation, estrogen, or atypical antipsychotics.

Wellbutrin-SR is often added to an SSRI such as Prozac, Paxil, or Zoloft and may offset sexual side effects of those three and may give additional energy.

2. *Antidepressants combined.* Since the SSRIs only work to increase the neurotransmitter serotonin, it makes sense that the addition of another antidepressant that also increases the level of other neurotransmitters such as norepinephrine or dopamine may help.

Thus, Wellbutrin-SR (a presynaptic dopamine-blocking agent that increases dopamine in the synapse) is added to an SSRI at times. Also, Remeron (mirtazapine) has at times been added to an SSRI. Remeron is what is known as a duel agent. It works to increase both serotonin and norepinephrine, which may be powerful in increasing mood. Remeron has various interesting mechanisms of action: it blocks two subdivisions of serotonin on the post receptor side and by so doing it may decrease sexual dysfunction and nausea. Remeron also blocks the reuptake of histamine at the presynaptic terminal and this result may help with insomnia. Of course, most medicines can have side effects and a common side effect of Remeron is weight gain. However, weight gain is desirable in some conditions (anorexia nervosa).

Another dual agent is Effexor-XR. It too results in an increase in both serotonin and norepinephrine. Effexor-XR has at times been combined with Wellbutrin-SR and at times with Serzone. Serzone (Nefazodone) has also been combined with Visken (pindolol) at times for a possible fast response onset in refractory depressions. Effexor-XR has also been combined with Wellbutrin-SR or Remeron. One is always concerned about possible drug interactions but in general, Effexor-XR, Remeron, Clexa, and Wellbutrin-SR may be less worrisome overall in this regard. It may be that Effexor-XR, Remeron, Clexa, and Serzone all decrease anxiety also.

3. *Antidepressant plus minor tranquilizer.* Some strategies have included combining an SSRI with BuSpar (buspirone), a partial post receptor serotonin antagonist at 5HT1A. BuSpar is a nonaddicting, antianxiety, minor tranquilizer. Other plans have included the addition of Xanax (Alprazolam), a benzodiazepine (minor tranquilizer) with an antidepressant. In some of the literature, it seems that Xanax alone may have an antidepressant effect. Of course, the issue of tolerance is a consideration.

4. *Antidepressant plus neuroleptic.* Another augmentation strategy that is being used is the addition of a new neuroleptic postsynaptic dopamine antipsychotic (Zyprexa/Olanzapine) with a standard antidepressant. It may have an antidepressant element because of its postsynaptic antagonism of a subdivision of serotonin (5H2). It may be that Risperdal (another new antipsychotic medication) may have antidepressant effects.

267

Another strategy that has been used is the addition of a relatively new antiseizure medication to the antidepressants. Lamictal/Lamotrigine may have antidepressant effects as well as mood stabilizing effects. Unfortunately, it can have serious side effects at times. Of course, almost any medicine can affect almost any organ so one must weigh the benefit/risk ratio. Also, Neurontin may be added in hopes of decreasing anxiety, insomnia, social phobias, and neuropathic pain. Neurontin is lower many times on drug interactions and has fewer side effects.

5. *Antidepressant plus estrogen.* It should also be mentioned that at times estrogen is being added to antidepressants in premenopausal women. Again, the benefit/risk ratio must be weighed since some women may have increased cancer risks (such as breast cancer) with estrogens. Estrogen levels may affect the neurotransmitter serotonin and this may explain depression issues with PMS, postpartum, and menopause. Estrogen is usually combined with progesterone to decrease the likelihood of endometrial hyperplasia.

## Bipolar Disorders

Lithium, a natural salt, was introduced in the treatment of mood swings in 1949. Over the years, it has been used the most in bipolar disorders.

Depakote has been approved for treatment of bipolar disorders. It may have overall less side effects than lithium, but it too can have potentially dangerous side effects.

Another antiseizure medication that has been used in treating bipolar disorders (although not technically approved for this) is Tegretol (possible side effects are also a concern here). Also, as an augmentation agent, Neurontin has been used as has Lamictal (neither technically approved for bipolar, but used as a matter of practice by many psychiatrists).

Also, Zyprexa (a neuroleptic) is being studied for its possible mood stabilizing effects, and, it has been suggested that Omega 3 fatty acids that are natural are usually well tolerated, often nontoxic, and may enhance mood stabilization. These studies will be interesting to watch.

## COMMON MEDICATIONS USED IN PSYCHIATRY

| | |
|---|---|
| Wellbutrin-SR/Bupropion-SR | Depakote/Valproic Acid |
| Effexor-XR/Venlafaxine-XR | Neurontin/Gabapentin |
| Remeron/Mirtazapine | Tofranil/Imipramine |
| Serzone/Nefazodone | Sinequan/Doxepin |
| Celexa/Citalopram | Vivactil/Protriptyline HCl |
| Xanax/Alprazolam | Tegretol/Carbamazepine |
| Prozac/Fluoxetine | Lithobid or Eskalith/Lithium |
| Paxil/Paroxetine | Lamictal/Lamotrigine |
| Zoloft/Sertraline | Topamax/Topiramate |
| Desyrel/Trazodone | Seroquel/Quetiapine |
| Luvox/Fluvoxamine | Dexedrine/Dextroamphetamine |
| Klonopin/Clonazepam | Elavil/Amitriptyline |
| Zyprexa/Olanzapine | Pamelor/Nortriptyline HCl |
| Risperdal/Risperidone | |

The symptoms of depression are multifactional. The causes are diverse and incorporate generalized current stressors, early life issues, and the choices one makes. The treatments are often excellent. There is much hope today for treating depression. Why not avail oneself of that help—medically, psychologically, and most of all, spiritually? Why not do something to get well? Aristotle once said that we are what we repeatedly do. This book presents the information that is usually considered among the best scientific and spiritual tools available today that will allow one to understand and change what one does—to go from depression to mood stability.

> Why art thou cast down, O my soul? and why art thou disquieted within me? hope thou in God: for I shall yet praise him, who is the health of my countenance, and my God. (Ps. 42:11 KJV)

# ABOUT THE AUTHORS

**Paul Meier, M.D.,** is cofounder of the New Life Clinics, one of the largest mental health care providers in the United States. He is the author or coauthor of more than forty books, including *Love Is a Choice, Windows of the Soul, Don't Let Jerks Get the Best of You, Love Hunger,* the *Mega-Millennium Series* and *The Secret Code.*

**Stephen Arterburn, M.Ed.,** is cofounder and chairman of the New Life Clinics. He is currently host of the New Life Clinics radio program. He is the author or coauthor of more than eighteen books, including *Winning at Work Without Losing at Love* and *The Power Book.*

For the New Life Clinic nearest you call 1-800-NEW-LIFE. To order a thirty-minute *Mastering Your Moods* video from Dr. Meier on the complete biopolar spectrum, call 1-800-NEW HOPE.

**Frank Minirth, M.D.**, is a board-certified psychiatrist and the President of the renowned Minirth Clinic in Richardson, Texas. Dr. Minirth co-hosts the Minirth Clinton Life Talk national radio program, broadcasted on the internet at MINIRTH-CLINIC.COM, and has authored and co-authored more than forty books including *Miracle Drugs, Love Is a Choice,* and *The Headache Book.*

For more information about the Minirth Clinic or to order a Mood Disorders audio tape from Dr. Minirth call **888-MINIRTH.**